Greatest Of All Time

Written by
Simona Piscioneri

Illustrated by
James Kennedy

Greatest Of All Time

Published by:
The Good Book Company

thegoodbook.com | thegoodbook.co.uk
thegoodbook.com.au | thegoodbook.co.nz

Design by André Parker | Illustrations by James Kennedy

ISBN: 9781802543520 | Printed in India

"Our generation needs this book and a hundred more like it! Clear, simple and accessible, it equips kids to interact with their God and his word in engaging ways."

ADAM GRIFFIN, Host, Family Discipleship Podcast

"I love it! Fun, faithful and accessible, this is a brilliant guide for kids to begin their solo Bible adventures with Jesus—the G.O.A.T."

AMY SMITH, Resource Writer, Faith in Kids

"Rich theology in a book your kids will want to pick up—*Greatest Of All Time* is a rare find! Written in a style that kids will relate and respond to, this resource reminds them that Jesus is the best there's ever been and that they can make their lives count by chasing hard after him. My boys loved it, and your kids will too."

ERIN DAVIS, Author, Bible teacher and mom

"A wonderfully engaging journey exploring Jesus—his amazing life, words, works and ways. The format is fun, interactive and personal. It includes backstory for each Bible passage, brilliant personal applications and a weekly round-up that draws everything together. I cannot think of a better resource to help kids aged 7-12 (and beyond!) take their next steps of faith."

TIM PIESSE, National Director, Building a Discipling Culture

"*Greatest Of All Time* is brilliant and includes all the things I look for in a great children's resource! Piscioneri has created what many set out to do but few have accomplished: a children's discipleship resource that is biblically grounded and theologically robust, yet easily approachable for kids of all ages. I cannot wait to get this into the hands of my children!"

CHRIS AMMEN, Founder, Kaleidoscope Kids' Bibles;
Author, *Raising Disciples at Home*

"I'm buying this book for my grandsons! Simona Piscioneri has written an interactive book which will capture their imagination and teach them about Jesus. The book is simple, fun and informative. Love it!"

JOHN FINKELDE, Founder, Grow a Healthy Church

"A fantastic devotional that helps kids and families discover the incredible life and love of Jesus. With fun illustrations, real-life connections and powerful truth, it invites readers to grow in faith and friendship with the one who is truly the Greatest Of All Time! Spending time with Jesus like this will shape hearts, strengthen faith and bring joy to the journey."

MR CHAD, Principal, Devonport Christian School, Tasmania

"*Greatest Of All Time* gave me more of a connection to Jesus and showed me how awesome Bible times were. My favourite thing about it was that I got to know Jesus more!"

JETHRO, aged 10

"My favourite thing about *Greatest Of All Time* is how interactive it is. It's easy to follow, has wonderful illustrations and is perfect for learning more about Jesus. I loved that I could read it quickly, yet still learn and absorb the information."

BRONTE, aged 12

"I really enjoyed learning about Jesus and the interactive parts of the book. I just think that people who want to find out and learn about Jesus should read this book!"

ANNABELLA, aged 11

"I enjoyed reading the Bible more and getting to know all of what Jesus did in his life. You should definitely buy this book!"

TAYLAR, aged 10

"This book is incredible! It helps you learn more about what Jesus did in the Bible, with great illustrations and easy ways to respond."

ANNABELLE, aged 11

Contents

Welcome!

In this book you'll get to know the Greatest (Person) Of All Time: God's Son, Jesus.

You probably know already how special Jesus is. There has never been anyone else in history who could do all the things he did! But the more time you spend finding out about the G.O.A.T., the more you'll see that surprisingly, he was also a lot like **YOU!**

Jesus often faced difficult choices and personal challenges, like being misunderstood, snoozing at unfortunate moments, and having friends who let him down. Sound familiar?

The way Jesus responded in those situations, the way he treated people, the unexpected things he sometimes said and did… these can teach us how to be more like him. We can live **OUR** best life—through the awesome moments **AND** the not-so-awesome ones—by following the example of the Greatest Of All Time: Jesus.

Getting The Most Out Of This Book

G.O.A.T. is a devotional book. That means it's a book to help guide your time with God. The best way to use it is to set aside a little time every day to read one short chapter.

There are five regular chapters per week, plus a reflection page for the weekend. (But it's okay if you don't always complete one week's worth of chapters in one actual week.)

Each day has a Bible passage for you to look up, plus thoughts, prayer prompts, and spaces to write or draw.

On the weekend round-up page, you'll find a quiz, plus opportunities to write down what stood out to you during the week. When you look back at these pages later, you might be surprised at how much you've learnt!

ONE MORE THING: You can also get an audio version of *Greatest of All Time!* Just head to thegoodbook.com/alltime-audio.

How To Look Up A Bible Verse

The Bible is the Greatest *Book* Of All Time, but it's also **VERY** large! Just in case you're not used to finding Bible verses yourself, here's a quick guide:

1. **FIND THE CONTENTS PAGE** (or it might be called Index) near the front of the Bible. The books of the Bible are divided into two sections: the Old Testament and the New Testament. The New Testament starts with the life of Jesus, so most of the books you'll be looking for will be in that section.
2. **LOOK FOR THE NAME** of the book, such as "Mark". If it's a person's name, it's often because that person wrote it. Find the page number that the book starts on and turn to it.
3. **WITHIN EACH BOOK** there are chapters and verses. Each chapter has a different number of verses. The chapters are shown first in the Bible passage you are looking up. For instance, Mark 1:2 means you are looking for the book of Mark, the first chapter and the second verse. The verse numbers are often printed in a really small size, so don't miss them!

Now you're set!

The beginning of the good news about Jesus the Messiah, the Son of God.

Mark 1:1

Week 1
Jesus Did Surprising Things When He Was Young

Have you ever thought that Jesus was once **EXACTLY** the same age you are now? It might seem strange to think that Jesus was like you in some ways, but it's true.

It's also true that Jesus is very **DIFFERENT** to you. When Jesus was born as a baby, that was the start of his earthly life, but he actually existed with God before that... forever! And the differences don't stop there.

Jesus' birth fulfilled prophecies and promises from God. You see, for many years, God had promised to send someone amazing—someone who would bring peace and rescue his people. The name for the promised person was "the Messiah", and we'll see that right from the beginning, Jesus was this promise fulfilled.

1. Jesus Changed Places

Have you ever dreamt of going somewhere completely different for a holiday? Perhaps if you live in a cold climate you'd like to go to a tropical island? Or you might like to leave the city to go exploring in the countryside?

When you imagine visiting another place, it probably seems much, **MUCH** better than where you actually live. Who would want to visit somewhere that was worse? Well, that's what Jesus did!

Bible time: Read Luke 2:4-14

This is the story of when Jesus was born, and you might think you know it. Don't miss the details.

Which two places were impacted when Jesus was born (v 14)?

The backstory: The backstory of Jesus coming to earth is him living in heaven. That's right: the jewel-encrusted buildings, the streets of gold, angels worshipping God non-stop… That perfect place where nothing bad happens, **THAT** was Jesus' home.

But Jesus swapped living in heaven with living on earth. He left heavenly perfection for a stinky, hay-filled manger where animals feed. And that's not all!

Dig deeper: Jesus didn't only downgrade his address. He became human. Even though he was still fully God, Jesus now had real, human limitations that he didn't have before. He was born as a tiny baby, and one day he would die.

Why the excitement? There was a lot of excitement in heaven when Jesus was born. A massive angel choir sang with joy to let the shepherds know this was a big deal. But why were they so excited that Jesus had left **THE** perfect home in heaven to be born as a helpless baby on earth?

The angels give it away when they call Jesus "the Messiah". You might know that title as one of the names of Jesus. But to anyone from God's family, the Jews, this was **AMAZING** news! The Messiah had been promised from God for generations—a chosen one who would save God's people. And **FINALLY** he's here! **RIGHT NOW!!!!**

Good news! Jesus being born is great news for us, but it's great news in heaven too. That's because it was always part of God's plan that Jesus—the Messiah—would come to earth. The angels celebrated, not because changing places was easy or fun for Jesus, but because he did it to complete God's plan to save us. This was God's promise being fulfilled. Angels couldn't help but celebrate!

Imagine that: Sketch a picture of something you might see in heaven. That's what Jesus left behind to fulfil God's plan to save us.

Prayer prompt: Say thank you to Jesus for being willing to change places so that he could be our Saviour.

2. Jesus Fulfilled Prophecy

Did you know that there are over 300 prophecies about Jesus as the Messiah in the Bible, and many of them were written down hundreds of years before he was even born? **WOAH!**

Prophecy? A prophecy in the Bible is a message from God, usually about something that would happen in the future. God used people called prophets to deliver these messages.

Of course, the prophecies about "The Messiah", God's promised rescuer, didn't have Jesus' name on them. They were more like clues to recognise him by. Only a few people at the time were given a clear message from God that **JESUS** was the Messiah whom God had promised. Let's meet one of those people.

Bible time: Read Luke 2:25-33

What two things does Simeon do in verse 28?

The backstory: God had told Simeon through his Holy Spirit that the Messiah would come in his lifetime. What a special promise! We don't know how old Simeon was when he met Jesus, but we do know that he recognised the Messiah immediately.

What happened? When Simeon was holding baby Jesus, he said some interesting things about him—in fact, this was a prophecy as well! Simeon didn't admire how cute the baby was or try to decide which parent he looked like. Instead, he thanked God for a little baby he had never seen before and called him a **LIGHT** and our **SALVATION**.

If Jesus was an ordinary baby, that would be very unusual! But Simeon is telling us that Jesus isn't ordinary.

What does it mean? Salvation and Saviour both come from the word "save". Even as a baby, the most important thing that Jesus would do—dying on the cross to save us from our sin—was part of his identity.

Simeon also prophesied that Jesus would be a light. Light is very useful because it helps us see. Jesus would grow up to help us see what God is like.

Why does it matter? What's the importance of Jesus fulfilling these prophecies in the Bible? It reminds us that when God makes a promise, he keeps it. He promised to send the Messiah, a Saviour, a rescuer, a light to point us to God, and he did!

Prayer prompt: God's Holy Spirit revealed who Jesus was to Simeon. Ask God for his Holy Spirit to reveal Jesus to you through this book!

Reflect: Draw a picture of a light shining and add the words "The Lord is **MY** light", or something else you want to say about Jesus.

3. Jesus Was Born A King

Have you ever imagined yourself as royalty? Perhaps when you were younger you would dress up as a princess in a tiara or swish a toy sword around and pretend you were a knight. Of course, even though it was fun, dressing up didn't make you a real member of the royal family.

When Jesus was born, some people he had never met before recognised that he was royalty. They travelled a long way to honour him as king.

Bible time: Read Matthew 2:1-12

How did King Herod feel when he found out another king had been born in his kingdom?

Historically speaking: Usually, when a baby is born into a reigning royal family, that child inherits the title "prince" or "princess". But did you notice that Jesus was "born king" (Matthew 2:2)? That's **VERY** unusual! (Especially since there was already a king in that region.)

What happened? It's not surprising that the wise men went to a palace to search for a king... But they didn't find the king they were looking for.

It was only when some Jewish teachers looked up a prophecy in the Bible about the Messiah that they found out the **NEW** king would be born in the small town of Bethlehem and not in a palace at all!

What kind of king? Jesus' parents, Mary and Joseph, were definitely not royalty. In fact, they were quite poor.

But Jesus is also the Son of God—that's why he's a king. His kingdom isn't a portion of land with a fancy castle. God's kingdom brings God's reign—his love, his justice, his power. God's kingdom came in the person of King Jesus!

Check the facts: Look again at the Bible verses in Matthew, and write down where each royal clue is found.

- The wise men followed a star showing them that a special new king had been born. They came a long way to honour him!
- King Herod was threatened by the news of a different king, even a baby one.
- The prophecy came true about God's rescuer, the Messiah, being born in Bethlehem.

- The wise men bowed down and gave expensive gifts to honour a very important person. These weren't gifts for a baby to play with, but gifts for a king.

Think about it: Jesus was a threat to King Herod, a prophecy come true from the Bible, a king to the wise men. Who is Jesus to you?

A royal response: What does it mean if Jesus is our king? It means we should be like the wise men and honour him. That means inviting Jesus to be in charge of our hearts and our lives.

Prayer prompt: Write a prayer that honours Jesus or names him as your king. *Dear Jesus, you are…*

4. Jesus Escaped A Death Threat

You may hear on the news about wars or natural disasters that sometimes happen around the world. When people's lives are in danger, they often pack up a few possessions and quickly move their family to another country to find safety. People who take refuge in another country are called refugees.

Jesus was a refugee. And the threat on his life was very real.

Bible time: Read Matthew 2:12-16

This story follows on immediately from yesterday as the wise men return home. King Herod is now **WAY** past being upset.

How is he described in verse 16?

The backstory: King Herod was known in history to be an unreasonable person. He even killed some of his own family so they couldn't steal his throne. So, threatening to kill this "other" king was nothing new for him, even if Jesus was just a baby.

What happened? When the angel spoke to Joseph in a dream, he obeyed immediately. Imagine how confusing and frightening it must have been! In the middle of the night, Joseph and Mary had to suddenly pack up and leave their home, relatives, and country—running away just to stay alive.

Mary and Joseph probably didn't understand everything that was happening, but they trusted that God had a plan. We can tell that by the way they did what God told them to do.

Why was it so hard? Just like in our present-day society, things happened in Jesus' life that were hard and difficult to understand. Maybe you thought life would have been easy for Jesus? After all, he was God's Son.

Jesus **WAS** God's Son—but he was living in a broken and sinful world. While his birth was surrounded by great joy and celebration, there was a sad part to it too. Other baby boys in Bethlehem died, and Jesus spent his first few years as a refugee in a foreign country.

Look ahead: This story about Jesus **NOT** dying is an important reminder that God had a plan, and no one could stop it.

You see, one day, many years later, Jesus **WOULD** die. That was God's plan too. And Jesus would **CHOOSE** to go through with it. Why? Because his death had a much bigger purpose than satisfying a jealous king. More about that in later chapters!

Think about it: Jesus didn't have an easy life just because he was God's Son. But he (and his parents) trusted God in the difficult situations.

Prayer prompt: Think of a challenging situation in the world or someone you know who is having a tough time. Perhaps it's you. Write a prayer to ask for help to trust that God has a plan, even when things are hard.

5. Jesus Got Separated From His Parents

Have you ever lost track of time? You know how it is—you're enjoying a game so much that you are completely surprised when the end-of-lunchtime bell rings, or your technology turn is over, or it's getting dark.

That happened to Jesus too, but it was his **PARENTS** who noticed he had lost track of time... Three days later!

Bible time: Read Luke 2:41–52

Was Jesus older or younger than you in this story?

The backstory: Jesus lived in a little village, but every year he visited the big city of Jerusalem with his parents. The city would have been buzzing with busyness as Jews came from every direction to celebrate the Passover Festival.

What happened? Sometimes this story is told as though Jesus got lost in the big city, but he didn't. Jesus knew exactly where he belonged.

As the family left Jerusalem to go home, Jesus' parents thought he was travelling with other family or friends. They had been travelling as a group, and that was pretty normal. The only thing was, by nighttime, a **WHOLE DAY'S** journey out of Jerusalem, Jesus was nowhere to be found. Uh-oh.

Talk about stressful! Finally, three days later, Mary and Joseph found Jesus in the temple. But twelve-year-old Jesus wasn't upset or missing his parents. He was **LOVING** being in God's house and having conversations about the Bible. In fact, he asked his parents why they thought he would be anywhere else.

Did he really...? Did Jesus just backchat his parents? No. Check verse 48. Mary says, "Your father and I have been anxiously searching for you", but Jesus reminds Mary that the reason he came to earth was to do what his **HEAVENLY** Father wanted. And because Jesus is God's Son, even when he was twelve he knew exactly what that was. **WOW!**

What does it mean? Why is this one story about Jesus' childhood included in the Bible?

What Jesus did always points us to who Jesus is. He was confirming his identity: he is not just the son of human parents but also the Son of God. His understanding of the Bible amazed the teachers in the temple. His special relationship with his heavenly Father stunned his earthly parents.

Think about it: Jesus was so sure that he belonged in God's house. He was certain that he could trust God's word and that he would never be separated from his heavenly Father. If we trust in God, we can be sure of these things too.

Prayer prompt: *Thank you God that I can be sure about...*

Becoming like Jesus: Like twelve-year-old Jesus, we can dive into God's word, the Bible. Unlike twelve-year-old Jesus, we may need help to fully understand it!

Who can you ask for help if you have a question about the Bible?

Week 1 Round-Up: A Big Beginning

Let's recap Jesus' early life with a quick quiz.

1. Who did the angels declare baby Jesus to be on Day 1?
2. The wise men gave Jesus a different, royal title. Jesus wasn't born a prince, he was born a…?
3. On Day 4 we met Simeon, who was waiting for God's promised Messiah. What did Simeon call Jesus?

What's something important you learnt about Jesus this week?

What will you do to make that thing part of your life too?

The names of Jesus point to his identity as God's Son, the promised Messiah. Can you think of any other names or titles that Jesus is called in the Bible? **Look up Isaiah 9:6 to find some.** Add them to the shapes below!

Write a prayer and talk to God about something that's happened in your week or that's coming up in the week ahead.

“The time has come,” [Jesus] said. “The kingdom of God has come near.”

Mark 1:15

Week 2
Jesus Launched His Mission

Jesus grew from a child into an adult, just like you will. But he never intended to settle into a regular life. Jesus came to earth on a mission to save the world, and when he was around 30 years old, the time came to launch that mission!

So, Jesus needed to introduce himself! The very first things he did announced who he is and why he came. But they also help us get to know Jesus as a person.

You see, even though Jesus was God's Son, launching this mission wasn't easy. There were challenges as well as successes. So, the start of Jesus' public ministry not only shows us what Jesus did but reveals his character while he did it.

Get ready to launch!

1. Jesus Was Baptised By His Cousin

Among your extended family, do you have any cousins or relatives of a similar age, who you get along with really well? Or maybe your cousins are completely different to you, and you find it a bit awkward when you spend time together.

Jesus had extended family too, including one quirky cousin called John—otherwise known as John the Baptist. They were about the same age and **BOTH** of them had a mission to tell people about God.

Bible time: Read Matthew 3:13-17

Draw a picture of Jesus' baptism based on verse 16.

The backstory: John was a preacher who told people to turn back to God, because the Messiah was coming. People were baptised (dunked under the water) to show that they were sorry for their sin and they wanted to say yes to being fully committed to God.

Enter Jesus: Jesus was about to fulfil John's message and let people know that he, Jesus, **WAS** the Messiah. He didn't need to say sorry for his sin, because he never sinned. But he did need to publicly declare his **YES** to God. One of the ways he did that was to get baptised.

But why? As Jesus' cousin, John knew all about Jesus being the Son of God. So, he was a bit confused as to why Jesus would want to be baptised by him (v 14). Shouldn't it be the other way around?

Here are some things we can learn from Jesus' baptism:

- Jesus was declaring his full commitment, his **YES** to God.
- God was happy about it! He said so!
- People saw God's Holy Spirit—on this occasion in the form of a dove—come upon Jesus after he was baptised. That showed that God's power and presence was with Jesus.
- Jesus already knew he was God's Son, but now lots of other people would know it too. His obedience in baptism, the voice of God the Father, the presence of the Holy Spirit—all these things would help prepare people to believe in Jesus. What a great way to launch his mission as Saviour of the world!

Becoming like Jesus: We can be like Jesus when we say yes to God. Sometimes, our yes leads to big moments, like getting baptised. Other times, our everyday yes to God means obeying him in much more ordinary ways.

What's something you can do to obey God and say **YES** to him today? Include it in your prayer below.

Prayer prompt: *Dear God, I want to say yes to you. I will…*

2. Jesus Skipped Dinner Once Or Twice

Can you remember a time when you were so excited that you were practically **BUZZING?** Perhaps you achieved a personal milestone like performing on stage, or your team won their grand final. Maybe you visited somewhere you've always wanted to go. We all have those **EXTRA** exciting moments, but sometimes, our emotions settle down afterwards with a bit of a thud.

Jesus has just had a **BIG** moment, getting baptised to obediently fulfil God's plan, and getting a huge pat on the back for it from God! Then... **THUD!** Now he's heading straight into a challenge.

Bible time: Read Luke 4:1-4

Jesus might not have had anything to eat, but what was he "full of" instead?

Did you catch that? Jesus was fasting, which means he went without food for a while... 40 days, in fact. That's over a month of **CHOOSING** to skip breakfast, lunch and dinner! (Yes, really!) He probably drank water during that time, but it is a **VERY** long stretch to go without food.

Did you notice that Jesus had company while he was fasting? Just to make things even harder! We'll go into more detail about Jesus' conversation with the devil in tomorrow's notes.

The backstory: Fasting has a long history in the Bible. It's when you choose to go without food for a while to focus on God instead.

Good preparation? Like it would for us, going without food made Jesus physically weak and hungry. That might not seem like a good way to launch into full-time teaching and healing! But Jesus knew there was something he needed even more than food, if his ministry was going to be a success. He needed God!

Look again at verse 4. Jesus quotes part of a verse from the Old Testament, saying, "Man shall not live on bread alone". The rest of that verse says, "...but on every word that comes from the mouth of the LORD" (Deuteronomy 8:3b).

Going without food meant Jesus had to **COMPLETELY** trust God his Father to take care of him. Even though fasting made Jesus' body physically weak, it made him spiritually even stronger.

Think about it: Is there something you could give up for a short period of time, and instead, focus on reading your Bible or praying, so you can become spiritually stronger? Perhaps you could miss a turn on technology one afternoon, or a snack? (Fasting meals is not recommended for children.)

Prayer prompt: Draw a picture of your favourite food and say thank you to God for it. Ask God to help you enjoy time with him as much as you enjoy that tasty treat.

3. Jesus Was Tempted To Do Wrong

Have you ever been tempted to do something you know is wrong? If we are truthful, the answer is going to be yes. Sometimes we can convince ourselves that our choices are just a little bit bad, or that what we did doesn't matter because no one will notice.

That wasn't Jesus' attitude. He was tempted but he **NEVER** sinned. Never sinning is something you and I can't do—we're not perfect like Jesus is! But we **CAN** learn from him about **HOW** to stop temptation in its tracks.

Bible time: Read Matthew 4:1-11

Remember yesterday's story? This is part 2 of what happened while Jesus was fasting. Write down one of the things the devil tried to get Jesus to do:

Was he really? Was Jesus actually tempted to do wrong? He's God's Son—was there ever a chance that he would give in?

Jesus' enemy, the devil, thought so. He deliberately came to Jesus when he was weak and hungry. He thought he could tempt Jesus away from God's plan, but he was wrong!

The devil tried three times to stop Jesus trusting completely in God. If Jesus had given in, he would have been following the devil's plan instead of God's plan. But Jesus said no, because his mission to become the Saviour of the world meant following **GOD'S** plan—all the way to the cross.

Enemy tactics: The devil (also called Satan) wants to destroy what God created. Jesus came to earth to create a solution to our sin problem forever, so of course the devil tried to wreck it. But don't worry, God is **WAY** more powerful than the devil!

Did you know? Did you realise that being tempted is not the same as sinning? When faced with temptation, we can choose not to give in, and instead do what's right. We can walk away. We can ask for help to make the right choice. We can do what Jesus did and remind ourselves of the truth in the Bible (and then do what the Bible says).

Buuuuut... because we're not perfect, sometimes we will give in to temptation and sin. The good news is that Jesus always forgives us when we are sorry for what we have done.

Tough stuff: Thinking about temptation can be pretty intense. Here's an encouragement for you: the Bible says God is on our side. He never tempts us to do wrong, so don't forget to ask for God's help! Look up 1 Corinthians 10:13 and write out your favourite part of this promise.

Prayer prompt:

Dear Jesus, I know I'm not perfect, like you are.

I'm sorry for ______________________________.

Please forgive me and next time help me see what the right choice is.

4. Jesus Spent Time Alone (Or Did He?)

What is something so important that you would get out of bed earlier than usual for it? Maybe it's a plane to catch or a family road trip or a special day that might involve gifts for you. Unless we have an exciting reason for it, getting out of bed extra early can be a bit of a chore.

I wonder if Jesus enjoyed getting up early?

Bible time: Read Mark 1:35

What was important enough to get Jesus out of bed super early?

Behind the scenes: Once Jesus started teaching and healing people of their sicknesses, it was very hard for him to find time alone. People literally tracked him down!

Alone time: Interestingly, when Jesus spent time alone, it was so he could be with God his Father. So, he was away from other people, but not really alone. In quiet conversations, Jesus could talk and listen to his Father, which prepared Jesus for what was coming up next.

Same same: Jesus developed a habit of spending time alone with God in prayer. That's probably not surprising considering he is God's Son. But this is something very cool for us to have in common with Jesus: Jesus **NEEDED** to pray.

If Jesus had a big decision to make (like choosing

his disciples), he spent time alone praying. (Look up Luke 6:12-16 if you want to see this for yourself.)

When Jesus did some of his miracles (like multiplying one boy's lunch to feed thousands of people), he prayed first (Luke 9:16-17).

When Jesus had the most difficult day of his life coming up, he poured out his emotions to God (Luke 22:39-44)!

Why pray alone? Jesus prayed a lot! It was kind of like he had a chat going with God all the time. But he also withdrew from other people, so he could prioritise one-on-one time with his Father. Just as it is for us, it was probably easier for Jesus to concentrate on listening to God in a quiet place, without extra noise and distractions. Alone-time prayer also helped Jesus deal with tricky emotions, and it helped re-energise him when he felt exhausted.

Becoming like Jesus: We can follow Jesus' example. We can chat to God our Father any time… but we can also plan to spend special alone time talking and listening to God.

Make a plan: Where will you have alone time with God? (Jesus liked to go outside, but inside works too.) What time of day will be best? (Super-early is not the only option!)

Prayer prompt: Take this book and a pen with you and write down what you ask/tell/thank God for in your special alone time with him.

5. Jesus Gathered A Support Crew

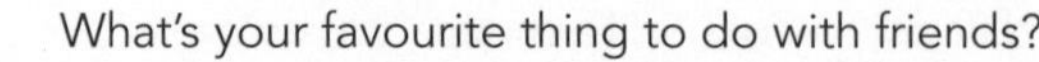

What's your favourite thing to do with friends? Chances are, you and your friends enjoy doing some of the same things. In fact, maybe you even became friends because you have something in common like playing in a team, or because you spend time together at church.

Jesus chose a group of twelve disciples who became his closest friends. They didn't have much in common at first, but spending time with Jesus became the thing that connected them.

Bible time: Read Luke 5:1-11

These fishermen are some of Jesus' first disciples. How much had Simon Peter caught before Jesus encouraged him to try again?

The gang: After experiencing this miraculous catch of fish, Simon, his brother Andrew, James and John left their boats to "follow" Jesus. That's a big deal! All the disciples left their jobs and their families to follow Jesus around the countryside, to learn from him, and live like him. That would have been hard, but also… **WOW!** Imagine being in Jesus' top twelve! The things these guys saw!!!

Did Jesus really need a team? As the Son of God, why did Jesus need ordinary people like fishermen to help him? Couldn't he have done it all on his own?

Jesus knew that he wouldn't be on earth forever. He taught his disciples how to follow him, so that later, they could teach others the same thing. (So **THAT'S** what "fishing for people" means in verse 10!)

But Jesus and his disciples became really good friends too. Did you realise that Jesus valued friendship just like you do?

Being a disciple: A disciple is a follower of Jesus. We can see in verse 5 that Simon already has one of the traits of a disciple: he said yes to Jesus! He had been fishing all night, but when Jesus told him to try again, he followed Jesus' instructions.

Did you know? Being a disciple of Jesus isn't just for people who met him in person 2,000 years ago. Anyone who follows Jesus by believing in him, learning from him and living like him can be his disciple. That includes you! And, just like Jesus' first disciples, when we spend time with Jesus and get to know him, he can become our closest friend too.

Prayer prompt: Jesus' disciples encouraged others to become disciples. Think of someone you know who isn't a follower of Jesus. Pray for them today, that they might become friends with Jesus. How could you share God's love with that person?

I'm going to pray for...

I could share Jesus with them by...

Week 2 Round-Up: Mission Launch Report

Let's recap Week 2 with a quick quiz.

1. What is one of the things Jesus did to show his obedience to God?
2. How did Jesus make sure he could really concentrate on talking and listening to God in prayer?
3. Why did Jesus choose to have a group of disciples instead of just doing everything on his own?

What's something important you learnt about Jesus this week?

What will you do to make that thing part of your life too?

We have focused this week on what Jesus did to launch his mission to become the Saviour of the world. One of these things, Jesus did over and over and over again throughout his life.

Look up Luke 5:16 and write down the who, what, where, when and why of this verse. **WHO** is this verse about? **WHAT** is happening? **WHERE**—what kind of place is it? **WHEN**—how often is this happening? And **WHY** is it happening? (The verse doesn't tell you the "why"—just write down what you think.)

Who?

What?

Where?

When?

Why?

Write a prayer and talk to God about something that's happened in your week or that's coming up in the week ahead.

“I have come that they may have life, and have it to the full.”

John 10:10b

Week 3
Jesus Offered People A Free Upgrade

Have you ever had a free upgrade? For example, you paid for a **MEDIUM**-sized burger-and-fries combo, but were given the **LARGE**, at no extra cost. (Winner!)

A free upgrade can be awesome, but it isn't usually a life-changing experience. When **JESUS** offered people a free upgrade, though, it often **DID** change their lives.

You see, the upgrade Jesus offered wasn't just for a bigger portion of the same thing. Sick people were healed. Unwelcome people were loved. Stressful situations that could have ended in disaster received a miracle instead.

And… you might be surprised to find out the **KINDS** of people who received the upgrade treatment from Jesus.

1. Jesus Gave Kids A High Priority

Which letter of the alphabet does your last name start with? If it's A, your name will be toward the top of most lists, because names are often sorted in alphabetical order. If your last name starts with Z, you might be used to waiting for your name to be called out last!

Sometimes, though, the list gets flipped, and those who are last get to go first. Jesus often "flipped the list" when it came to valuing people. For instance, his disciples didn't think kids were very important, but Jesus had other ideas!

Bible time: Read Mark 10:13-16

What did Jesus end up doing for the kids who were brought to him?

The backstory: The disciples weren't just being grumpy grown-ups when they tried to stop parents bringing their kids to Jesus. They were probably trying to guard his limited time for things **THEY** thought were more important, like preaching and healing people. In those days, most people didn't give children a very high priority.

Did he really? Did Jesus just tell his disciples to be more like... **YOU?** In verse 15, Jesus encouraged his disciples to "receive the kingdom of God like a little child". That means everyone should trust and depend on God, just like kids trust and depend on adults to take care of them.

Jesus "flipped the list"! To him, the kids weren't any less important than the adults—in fact, kids had something to **TEACH** the adults!

Words and actions: The thing about Jesus is, when he **SAID** something was important, he also followed it up with actions. When Jesus invited the children to come to him, he upgraded kids in importance. Then he made time to hug those random kids and bless them. That means he prayed especially for them. I wonder if they realised how significant that moment was.

An open invitation: The invitation for children to come to Jesus is still open. You may already know this, but you don't have to wait until you're older, or until you know more of the Bible, or until you feel like you deserve it. Jesus loves each unique person, and invites us all to come to him, no matter how young or old we are. (And yes, that even includes your younger siblings!)

Prayer prompt: Draw a simple portrait of yourself in the frame. Write a prayer of thanks to Jesus for how much he loves and values kids, including you.

2. Calling Doctor Jesus

When you are sick, you go to a doctor, who can diagnose what is wrong with you. Then, the doctor will let you know what to do to get better. If you ignore the doctor's advice, or pretend you aren't sick in the first place, there's a chance that you won't get well.

Did you know that Jesus once referred to himself as a doctor? Let's meet Levi, who got well after an appointment with Jesus—but he wasn't sick in the way we would usually think of it.

Bible time: Read Luke 5:27-32

What did Levi leave behind to follow Jesus?

The backstory: Levi (who is sometimes known as Matthew) was a tax collector before he met Jesus. Most Jewish people considered tax collectors to be traitors, because they collected money from their own people to pay to the Romans.

Why Levi? Why did Jesus invite a tax collector, who most people hated, to follow him? And then why did he go and eat with "sinners"? The religious leaders certainly wouldn't have done that!

Jesus spent time with all kinds of people—kids and adults, rich and poor, sick and healthy, those who had made bad choices and good ones... These were people from all walks of life who had something in common: they knew they **NEEDED** Jesus.

What kind of sickness? Jesus did many miracles that healed sickness in people's bodies. But Levi wasn't sick in the way we usually think of sickness. Look again at verses 31-32. Jesus diagnosed Levi with a sin problem. His symptoms included bad choices, hurting others and disobeying God. But Jesus came to heal people who knew they needed **HIM** to fix their sin sickness! People like Levi. People like **US.**

The turn-around: It might seem like leaving a well-paid job behind would make Levi's life worse, but when he accepted the invitation to follow Jesus, his life became much better. He welcomed Jesus into his home and his heart, and found the remedy for his sin sickness.

Who else is sick? If you have a sneaking suspicion that the answer is "All of us", then you'd be right! We **ALL** have a sin problem. We **ALL** need Jesus, who offers the only solution to spiritually heal us.

Prayer prompt: Spend some time talking with God about a sin problem you want to leave behind (like being selfish, or using disrespectful words, or being untruthful). You could include the words in your drawing below.

Reflect: Draw a picture of a heart or a band-aid plaster. Add the words "I need Jesus to…" and finish the sentence in your own words.

3. Jesus Saved A Party

What would be included in your best party ever? Whether it has a fun theme, or your favourite bunch of people, or an exciting venue, parties are celebrations that usually include plenty of food.

Now imagine if the food and fizzy drinks ran out just as you sat down to eat. Someone forgot to bring the cake, the only thing left to drink is water, and everybody else gobbled up the other goodies before you could get any! Is it still the best party ever?!

Jesus went to parties and celebrations too. On this occasion, there was a little bit of a problem…

Bible time: Read John 2:1-11

Who prompted Jesus to save this party?

A bit of history: In Jesus' day, weddings were big celebrations that could last up to a week. To run out of wine for the guests was a **HUGE** mistake! This would have brought embarrassment and shame on the family hosting the wedding party.

The conversation: When Jesus' mother, Mary, told him about the wine problem, Jesus responded with some unusual words. Back then, calling his mum "Woman" wasn't rude, even though it might be today!

The mum factor: As they were talking, Jesus gave Mary a reminder that his ministry was on God's timing and no one else's. Of course, Mary knew that Jesus was God's Son, and that he could do miraculous things, but perhaps she was keen for others to know it as well. (Side note: Jesus had a proud mum too!)

The miracle: Jesus instructed the servants to fill large water jars with water. Only the servants, Jesus' disciples and Mary knew what happened—the water turned into wine!

Jesus shows himself: Jesus' miracles reveal that he is God's Son. This miracle shows us his power, but also his **HEART.** Jesus cared about the wedding hosts so much that he gave them more wine to save the party… but even better than that, Jesus gave them finer quality wine than they had before! Even though turning water into wine didn't save anyone's life, it saved the family from humiliation.

Asking Jesus for help: Mary knew to turn to Jesus for help, and we can know that too. Jesus cares about what's going on in our lives, so we can talk to him about anything that's on our minds—whether it's big or small, life-changing or just embarrassment-saving.

Prayer prompt: *Dear Jesus, I know you care about what's happening in my life, even the little things. Please help…*

4. Jesus Turned An Interruption Into An Opportunity

Have you ever been jostled in a crowd? Maybe you've been to a huge concert or a sports event filled with cheering fans. Sometimes, when there is a **REALLY** large crowd of people, it's hard not to get squished, pushed around a bit, or trodden on.

Jesus experienced being pushed around in a crowd, but **HE** was the one that people were jostling to see!

Bible time: Read Luke 8:40-50

How did Jairus show that he was desperate to get Jesus' attention?

The interruption: On the way to saving the life of Jairus' daughter, Jesus pauses. In the middle of a crushing crowd, Jesus knows someone touched him—not by accident, but on purpose. Someone touched the edge of his cloak hoping to be healed… and Jesus knows it! **WOW!**

But he doesn't get grouchy at this interruption. Instead, Jesus waits for the person to come forward, and then praises the woman who reached out to him in faith.

What about Jairus' daughter??? While Jesus pauses to talk to the healed woman, Jairus finds out that his daughter has died. It all seems too late. How tragic!

But Jesus encourages Jairus to keep on trusting him.

Bible time: Read the end of the story in Luke 8:50-56

Different but the same: Let's compare these two stories of healing.

- Jairus was an important leader in the community, but we don't even know the name of the bleeding woman. Both of them were desperate for Jesus' help.
- Jairus begged Jesus in front of everyone to come and heal his daughter, whereas the woman tried not to make herself known. Both of them were scared, but they reached out to Jesus in faith.
- Jairus had to wait, while the woman jumped the queue for Jesus' attention. Both of them received the miracle healing they needed.

The opportunity: Jesus chose to turn this interruption into an opportunity to help more than one desperate person. He didn't need to rush or worry about how much time it took, because Jesus had the power to even bring Jairus' daughter **BACK TO LIFE!** Only Jesus could do that!

We should never think that reaching out to Jesus is a bother to him. We can invite him into our lives and into our difficult situations any time at all—it's never too late to ask! Remember, Jesus upgraded what most people would call an interruption, and turned it into an opportunity to help someone.

Prayer prompt: Ask Jesus to help you have faith like the people in today's Bible story.

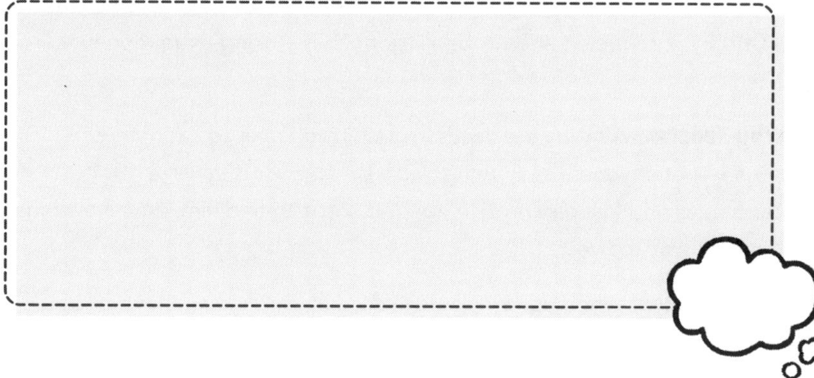

5. Jesus Gives People A Second Chance

Do you remember, when you were little, how everything seemed so much bigger than you? Maybe you used a step stool to reach up to the kitchen bench to "help" with cooking, or had a ride on someone's shoulders so you could see up ahead. Maybe you still feel like you're not quite tall enough to do everything you'd like to!

Today we meet someone who was too short to see over a crowd, so he climbed a tree in order to see Jesus. That sounds like a fun option for a kid, but it may have looked a little **STRANGE** when a grown man did it!

Bible time: Read Luke 19:1-10

Who invited Jesus to Zacchaeus' house?

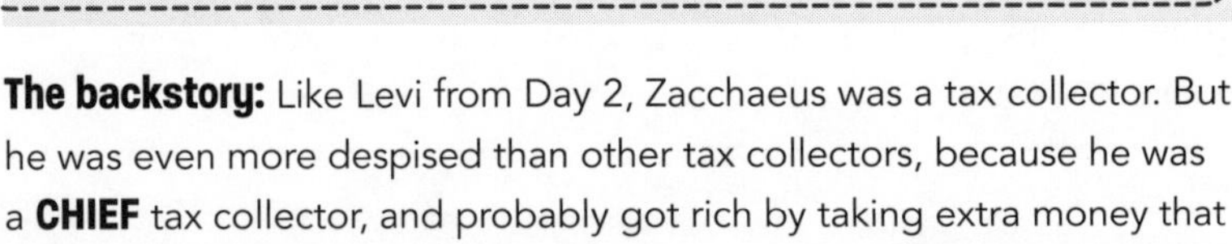

The backstory: Like Levi from Day 2, Zacchaeus was a tax collector. But he was even more despised than other tax collectors, because he was a **CHIEF** tax collector, and probably got rich by taking extra money that wasn't his.

Why Zacchaeus? Why did Jesus invite himself over to Zacchaeus' house—not anyone else in that town? The answer is in verse 10. Zacchaeus had lost his way. He needed Jesus to find him, and show him the right way to live.

Jesus notices: When other people looked at Zacchaeus, they saw a sinner who had stolen money to make himself rich. Jesus saw that too.

But Jesus looked beyond the bad things Zacchaeus had done—he saw the good person he could **BECOME.**

Jesus knew that Zacchaeus was ready to change his ways. Most people wouldn't befriend a tax collector, but Jesus showed him kindness and offered him a second chance. Zacchaeus accepted the opportunity to change, and it turned his life around completely!

Kindness is catching: It must have been hard for Zacchaeus to admit his mistakes, and to give back what he had taken. But it seems like Jesus' kindness rubbed off on Zacchaeus. He responded by giving back **FOUR TIMES** what he had stolen!

Think about it: None of us deserve Jesus' kindness, but in spite of our mistakes, he offers us the opportunity to change. He wants to be our friend and get to know us. How will we respond to the kindness he has shown us?

Imagine that Jesus found you in an unusual place, like up a tree. If he invited himself over to your place, how would you respond to him?

Prayer prompt: Just like Zacchaeus, we can upgrade our lives by becoming a friend and follower of Jesus. If you have never asked Jesus to be your friend and Saviour, but you would like to, turn to page 125 and use that prayer as a guide.

Week 3 Round-Up: Jesus Upgrades People's Lives

Let's recap this week with a quick quiz:

1. Did Jesus think that kids should or shouldn't come to him to be blessed?
2. What kind of party did Jesus save from humiliation?
3. We learnt about two tax collectors this week. How did most people treat tax collectors? How did Jesus treat them?

What's something important you learnt about Jesus this week?

What will you do to make that thing part of your life too?

Jesus upgraded the lives of all kinds of people who believed in him. That doesn't mean that their lives suddenly became easy. It means that when we get to know Jesus and trust him, say sorry for our sin and let Jesus change our hearts, it leads to the most fulfilling life we can have.

Look up John 10:10 and write the second half of the verse out here:

Write a word or phrase that starts with each letter below and that describes an upgraded and faith-filled life with Jesus.

L

I

F

E

Write a prayer and talk to God about something that's happened in your week or that's coming up in the week ahead.

"Everyone who hears these words of mine and puts them into practice is like a wise man who built his house on the rock."

Matthew 7:24

Week 4
Jesus Was Not Your Average Kind Of Teacher

Think about your favourite teacher ever. What was it about them that you liked?

Perhaps it wasn't so much **WHAT** they taught but the **WAY** they taught it that you remember. Or maybe it was their caring attitude, or the fact that they made learning fun.

Curious crowds of people were drawn to listen to the teachings of Jesus. What he taught **AND** the way he taught it… His teaching wasn't like anything they had ever heard before! It was challenging and surprising, and sometimes it even made people angry!

And yet what Jesus taught back then, still speaks to us today through the Bible. It's still important and still unique. Two thousand years later, the teachings of Jesus still show us the best way to live.

1. Jesus Told Good Stories

Do you enjoy reading a book from cover to cover? Or watching a movie through all the twists and turns, to find out what happens in the end? If you're someone who likes a good story, then you and Jesus have something in common.

But Jesus was no ordinary storyteller! He often told "parables"—stories with an extra meaning. A parable usually started like a regular story, but by the end, you'd learn an unexpected spiritual truth.

Bible time: Read Luke 8:4-8, then skip to verses 11-15

What does the seed represent in this parable?

In the dirt: Jesus talks about four different kinds of ground that the seeds land on. Not surprisingly, the good soil is the only type where healthy plants grow.

Of course, Jesus isn't really giving a farming lesson here. The different grounds represent our hearts, so let's look at each one more closely.

- Verses 5 & 12: **THE PATH.** This seed sits on the surface of the hard path. It's like someone who isn't interested in God's word at all. The message doesn't sink in.
- Verses 6 & 13: **THE ROCKY GROUND.** The seed starts to sprout, but the plant dries out because of the rocky soil. This is like people who give up on God when life gets tough.
- Verses 7 & 14: **THE THORNS.** The seed begins to grow, but thorns grow too, and eventually they choke it. This represents someone who

doesn't make God's word the most important influence in their life.

- Verses 8 & 15: **THE GOOD SOIL.** A seed grows into a healthy plant and produces a harvest. This is what Christians aim to do: to plant God's word in our hearts and grow our faith!

Sketch it: Draw a simple picture of each seed and ground scenario.

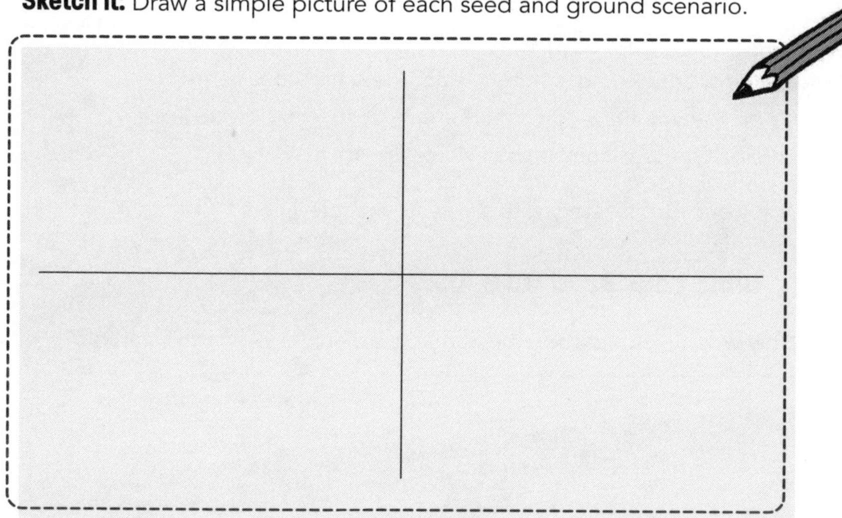

The challenge: Jesus didn't want people to just hear a good story—he wanted them to apply it to their lives! This story challenges us to keep our hearts open to receive God's word.

How can I improve the soil? What if you, or someone you know, has hard, rocky or weedy ground? The good news is that just as garden soil can be improved, so can the condition of our hearts!

Prayer prompt: *Dear Jesus, please make my heart like the good soil, ready to receive your word. I pray that your word will keep growing in my heart.*

PS: You can pray this every time you open up the Bible to read it!

2. Jesus Made The Bad Guy The Hero

What comes to mind when you hear the word "hero"? Perhaps you think of a person who does heroic deeds, like a firefighter rescuing someone from the dangerous flames. Or maybe you think of a superhero, with special powers like invisibility, super-human strength or the ability to fly.

Jesus once told a story with a very unexpected hero.

Bible time: Read Luke 10:29-37

How would you describe the Samaritan man, based on this parable?

Meet the characters: The characters that Jesus describes in this parable would have been familiar to all his listeners, but might not be obvious to us.

- The injured man: The victim of our story was robbed, beaten up and left for dead.
- The priest and the Levite: Both of these men saw the injured man and didn't stop to help… but they should have done. Their roles included special responsibilities from God to help those in need! But instead, they crossed the road to get away from the man who was hurt.
- The Samaritan: Our hero! A visitor from the nearby country of Samaria, this person showed incredible kindness to the hurt stranger and took excellent care of him.

Wait… **WHAT?**

When the baddie is the good guy: In a jaw-dropping twist that took everyone by surprise, Jesus made a Samaritan the hero of his story. A **SAMARITAN!!!** Jews and Samaritans had a bitterness toward each other that went back centuries. They **HATED** each other!

It's hard to explain how shocking Jesus' story would have sounded back then. Imagine your favourite superhero's arch-enemy saving the day—that's what this was like. What was Jesus trying to teach us by making an enemy the hero?

Who is my neighbour? In this parable, Jesus reminded the religious expert that being a neighbour is not about **WHERE** we live, but **HOW** we live: showing kindness, care, generosity and love to **ALL** those who come across our path, no matter who they are. We shouldn't be prejudiced against certain types of people. That's what Jesus shows us by making a Samaritan the hero of the story.

"Go and do likewise": This instruction from Jesus in verse 37 makes it clear that the good Samaritan's kindness is an example that we should follow.

What would it take for you to be the hero of this story? Do you notice when people need help? Do you offer to support others, even in small ways? This week, look for opportunities to offer your help or care, whether it's in the playground, the classroom or at home. You can be the kindness hero!

Prayer prompt: Ask Jesus to show you how you can help someone in need this week.

3. Jesus Broke The Rules

Rules, rules, rules! How do you feel about rules? Some rules are made to keep us safe, like speed limits for cars, or wearing a seatbelt. We know that breaking those rules can have serious consequences.

Then there are other rules. Maybe you have rules at home about how long you can spend on technology, or what time you go to bed. You may have mixed feelings about the importance of those rules!

Jesus and the Jewish religious leaders disagreed about the meaning of one of God's rules. Here's what happened…

Bible time: Read Matthew 12:9-14

What did Jesus do that caused such a stir?

The backstory: Way back in the Old Testament, God gave Moses ten commandments about how to live. One of them was to keep the seventh day of the week (the "Sabbath") as a day of rest and worship to God. There was to be no work on that day. You can read it for yourself in Exodus 20:8-11.

By the time Jesus was on earth, the Jewish leaders had made **LOTS** of extra rules about work on the Sabbath, but they had forgotten God's reasons for the rule.

Did Jesus break the law? When Jesus saw someone who needed help on that particular Sabbath, he couldn't ignore them. The Sabbath day was partly about what you **DON'T** do (like work), but it was also about what you **DO** do (like worshipping God)!

Some people thought that Jesus broke a rule that day, but Jesus interpreted the rules differently. He kept God's holy day special by valuing a person God had created and healing them with God's power. He used godly wisdom to teach us the true meaning of the rule.

So, about those rules... If Jesus didn't exactly follow the rules, does that mean that rules are out the window? No! Jesus followed lots of rules, like honouring his parents and paying taxes to the government. Because Jesus is God's Son, he knew what God's rules really meant, so we can be sure that Jesus got it right!

What does it mean for me? What Jesus chose to do that Sabbath day shows us God's heart. God does have rules that he wants us to follow, but more importantly he wants us to know his heart behind the rules.

If you are ever unsure of the right choice, think about who God is. He is loving, he is fair, he is holy. The more we find out about Jesus, the more we learn who God is, and the more we can be confident of making choices that honour God every day of the week.

Prayer prompt: Let God know that you want your choices to honour him today and every day. You might like to pray about a particular rule you find it hard to follow!

4. Jesus Asked Awkward Questions

Have you ever had a moment so awkward that you wished the ground would open up and swallow you whole? Like accidentally blurting out someone's birthday surprise. Or complaining about a teammate, only to realise you're talking to their best friend.

Although Jesus asked awkward questions sometimes, he never seemed embarrassed or unsure of what to do next.

Bible time: Read John 5:1-9

What is the awkward question that Jesus asked the man who couldn't walk?

Location, location: While Jesus was in Jerusalem, he specifically went to this place, the pool of Bethesda. It wasn't a swimming pool, though. Some people believed that the pool had healing powers, so lots of disabled people waited there, hoping for a chance to get well.

Awkward!!! It seems a bit rude to ask someone who had been sick for a really long time if they would like to get better. Surely the answer is obvious?

The disabled man knew he needed help, but his answer shows that he was hoping in the wrong thing to help him. He didn't need a mysterious pool or someone to push him into it, he needed **JESUS!**

Did he really? Did Jesus use his "teacher voice"? You know the one, when the teacher **REALLY** means it! Look again at verse 8. Jesus spoke with authority—that means he spoke like someone who was in charge.

And check out what happened! On the authority of Jesus, the man was cured. It wasn't because of the man's faith—he didn't know who Jesus was. It was all God's power, through his Son, telling the man to get up and walk.

"Pick up your mat": Jesus wasn't just being super tidy when he told the man to pick up his mat and go. The man's mat secured him a spot as an invalid at the pool, and made his difficult life a bit more comfortable.

Jesus was letting him know that he didn't **NEED** a place for his mat in the disabled area anymore. That was no longer his life, and he shouldn't go back to it. The man trusted the authority of Jesus and did what he said.

Think about it: Just like the man at the pool was hoping in the wrong thing to help him, sometimes we can do that too. Sometimes we focus on a problem or on waiting for someone to fix it for us, and don't even ask Jesus for help.

Sometimes, we really just need Jesus. What situation, big or small, do you need to trust to him?

Prayer prompt: Use your answer above to talk to God. Jesus has the authority to change our situation. We can trust him to do what's best.

5. Jesus Dished Out Hard Truth

Some people love the sound of rain on the roof. They find it comforting to know they are safely tucked up inside. But what if instead of being in a secure, warm house, you were out camping during a storm? The wind and rain against the flimsy walls of a tent are not quite as soothing!

Jesus once told a parable of two houses in a storm. But of course, there's more to the story than a whole heap of rain.

Bible time: Read Luke 6:46-49

According to Jesus, what is the difference between a well-built house and one that doesn't last?

Some building background: In case you've never realised, permanent buildings have a lot going on underground that we can't see. Before the walls go up, a builder must make sure the house is anchored to the ground. The important base-layer that the rest of the house is built on is called the foundation.

What are we building here? Although Jesus was originally a carpenter, this story **ISN'T** a building lesson... not a house-building lesson anyway. Jesus is talking about the foundation we build our lives on, and it's more than just **HEARING** Jesus' words.

Tough truth: Jesus wasn't satisfied just because a big crowd of people were listening to his teaching. He wanted them to put his words into practice. In fact, he seems to think that hearing his words and **NOT** putting them into practice is a waste of time.

This parable is also told in Matthew 7:24-27. In that retelling, Jesus describes someone who doesn't put his words into practise as "foolish". **OUCH.**

About that storm... Did you notice that the well-built house **AND** the foolishly built one were **BOTH** hit by a severe storm? So, even if we are wise, and build our lives on listening to and following Jesus' teaching, we may still get hit by difficulties (storms).

But here's the difference: if your life has that firm foundation, built on living out what God's word (the Bible) says, your faith will help you make it through the storm.

A question from Jesus: Look again at Luke 6:46. Could Jesus be talking to **YOU?** Are you willing to learn from him and do what he says? What might need to change to make that happen?

Prayer prompt: If Jesus is your Lord, commit to him that you want to hear his words and do them.

Your "house" plans: Draw a horizontal line through the middle of the box to the right. Under the line, draw a chunky foundation stone and write something like "living out God's word" in it. On top of the line, draw a house, and label it "my life".

Week 4 Round-Up: What To Learn From The Best Teacher Ever

Let's do a quick recap of Jesus' brilliant teaching from this week:

1. In the parable about farming, what does the seed represent?
2. In the parable about building, what should we build our lives on?
3. What Jesus said often surprised people. What unexpected thing did the Samaritan hero in Jesus' story do?

What's something important you learnt about Jesus this week?

What will you do to make that thing part of your life too?

Look up Matthew 7:28-29 and Mark 6:2 to find out more about Jesus as a teacher.

How did people feel about Jesus' teaching?

What was Jesus' teaching like?

Why was Jesus able to tell such interesting stories, answer tricky questions and ask even trickier ones? Because his wisdom came straight from God. He's not just a great teacher, he's God's Son! Jesus' unique teaching really challenged some people, and sometimes it challenges us. But because we know who Jesus is, we know his teaching is totally trustworthy.

Write a prayer and talk to God about something that's happened in your week or that's coming up in the week ahead.

Jesus looked at them and said, "With man this is impossible, but with God all things are possible."

Matthew 19:26

Week 5
Crazy Things Happened When Jesus Was Around

Have you ever seen a miracle? Not a magic trick, or something in a movie—have you ever experienced something you **REALLY** believe could only have happened because God did it?

Wherever Jesus went, he did miraculous things. Even his disciples, who knew Jesus best, were sometimes shocked when the impossible became possible.

A miracle is something so amazing that only God could do it. Apart from being incredibly helpful, the miracles of Jesus confronted people with a challenging thought: what kind of person can do something like **THAT?!**

1. Jesus Walked On Top Of Water

Have you ever seen an optical illusion? That's where a picture uses colours or patterns to convince your brain that what you're seeing is different to what it **REALLY** is. It's like it's playing a magic trick on your eyes.

I wonder if Jesus' disciples thought they were seeing an optical illusion, that dark, windy night on the lake…

Bible time: Read Matthew 14:22-33

What did the disciples say after Jesus got into the boat?

The backstory: At the end of the day, Jesus sent the disciples ahead of him to the next town across the lake, but they were having a rough time of it. They were rowing against the wind in the middle of the night and getting nowhere. They would have been wet and tired and maybe a little bit frustrated.

A surprise visitor: Then, in the middle of their exhaustion, a bleary-eyed disciple suddenly yells out in fright. Are his eyes playing tricks on him? In the dim light of dawn, something impossible is happening! How could someone be walking toward them in the middle of the lake? Is it a ghost?!?

That's too crazy! No—it's Jesus.

Walking. On. **TOP OF.** The. Water.

That's **IMPOSSIBLE!!!** How could they trust that it really was Jesus?

The trust test: One of Jesus' disciples, Peter, decided to put his faith to the test by getting out of the boat and walking on top of the water toward Jesus. At first his faith held him up, but when Peter got scared and started to sink, Jesus was right there to save him.

Lessons from Jesus: Jesus asks Peter in verse 31, "Why did you doubt?" The answer might seem obvious to us: people aren't meant to walk on water! But what's also obvious is that Jesus has power to do miracles. He was, and still is, the Son of God, and he **STILL** offers us opportunities to trust him. The best opportunities to trust Jesus often come in the trickiest situations.

Faith over fear: Even after being amazed by Jesus, Peter found it hard to trust him completely. Maybe that sounds familiar. Maybe fear is something you struggle with too. Even though you know Jesus is right there with you, you worry, or feel overwhelmed or fearful. Just like Peter discovered, we **CAN** trust Jesus in the middle of our fear.

Rewrite Jesus' words from verse 27, putting your name at the beginning, as though Jesus was talking directly to you.

Prayer prompt: Thank God that he can do amazing things that you can't do. Ask him to help you to trust him when things seem impossible. Ask him for faith instead of fear.

2. Jesus Read People's Thoughts

Have you ever played a board game and wished you knew what your opponent was going to do next? If you could see their cards or know their next move, then you could outplay them, and win! Apart from guessing, or cheating (I hope not!), there isn't really any way of **KNOWING** what someone else is thinking.

Unless you are Jesus.

Bible time: Read Luke 5:17-26

What did the man do after he was healed?

In the background: This is a story about Jesus miraculously healing someone who couldn't be healed by anyone else. That, on its own, is very cool.

But check out the other characters in the story. This paralysed man's friends were so determined to get him to Jesus that they pulled someone's roof apart to do it! What amazing friends! Jesus saw **THEIR** faith and the man was healed.

Then there were the teachers of the law. Their thoughts were angry and critical. Jesus saw what was in their hearts before they even spoke a word. Verse 22 says, "Jesus **KNEW** what they were thinking"! Wow!

Jesus stirs things up: Why didn't Jesus just ignore what the teachers of the law were thinking? Wouldn't that have been easier? Jesus actually used their negative opinions to prove his argument.

Look back at the Bible reading, noting the verse number next to each point.

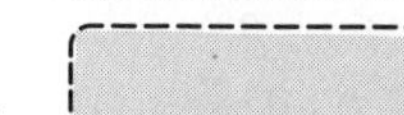

- The teachers of the law thought to themselves that only God has authority to forgive sin. They were right about that part.
- Jesus read their thoughts and said them out loud.
- Jesus says that **HE** has authority to forgive sin, as well as to heal.

So Jesus used the negative thoughts of his challengers to prove that he is… who?!

What does it mean for me? Jesus knows what's on **YOUR** mind too. He is God, after all. He still wants you to come to him with all your needs, like the paralysed man's friends did. Plus, you can bring your questions and uncertainty to Jesus too. That's a good thing to do! It was the teachers' disbelieving and negative **ATTITUDE** that Jesus challenged.

Prayer prompt: Think about the background characters in today's story: the friends who went to Jesus in faith, and the teachers of the law who criticised in their hearts.

If you ever find that you have an angry or questioning attitude toward Jesus, don't just churn it over in your heart. Be like the friends, who sought Jesus out to get his help.

Jesus knows what you're thinking. He loves you. He wants you to bring your needs, your praise and your questions to him. Talk to him now about what is on your heart.

3. Jesus Created The World

Have you ever imagined what it would have been like watching God create the world? Seeing the sun, the moon and the stars appear in the sky as God spoke them into existence. Witnessing all those animals splash, creep or roar to life. How absolutely incredible that would have been!

But hang on, what has creation got to do with Jesus? Wasn't he born thousands of years **AFTER** God created the world?

What has creation got to do with Jesus? **EVERYTHING!!!**

Bible time: Read John 1:1-3

When John talks about "the Word", he means Jesus.

Now read Genesis 1:1-3 (the very first verses in the Bible!)

They sound a little bit similar. Which phrase appears in both passages, and tells us **WHEN** Jesus' life really started?

What??!? Most of us make our entrance into the world when we are born as a baby, but Jesus' history goes further back than that. Waaaaay further back!

In a concept that can be hard to get our heads around, Jesus has existed forever as God (he was there "in the beginning")… **AND** he was born as a human baby at a certain moment in history, many years later. He is both fully God and fully human at the same time. **WOAH.** Even though this sounds like an impossibility, it's not impossible for God.

Unnamed: The book of Genesis doesn't mention Jesus by name when it tells us how the world was created, but because we know Jesus is God, we know he was there. Other parts of the Bible make it really clear that Jesus wasn't just standing by, watching God the Father create the world. Creation happened **THROUGH** Jesus! (You can explore this further by looking up Colossians 1:16 and Hebrews 1:2.)

Just another miracle? Like all the other miraculous things that happened through Jesus, creating the world took power that only God has. Sometimes we might get so familiar with the way Jesus healed people, or how often he did it, that we forget how enormously **SPECIAL** a miracle is.

Go looking: Sometime this week, go looking for signs of the Creator in the miracle of creation. Perhaps you will find it in a stunning sunset, or in the details of a spider's web in your backyard, or in a hug from someone you love. (God created people through Jesus too!)

Prayer prompt: Sketch something amazing that God has created, remembering that "in the beginning" Jesus was already there. Tell Jesus how much you appreciate the incredible world God created through him.

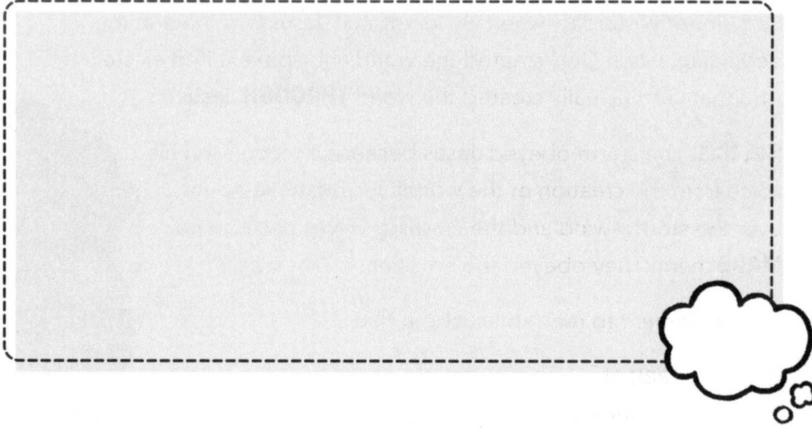

4. Jesus Talked To A Storm

Do you have a pet that is trained to follow instructions? It takes time to gain the love and respect of animals, to train them to listen to your voice. Perhaps, if you say, "Sit!" to your dog, it obediently does exactly that. Or perhaps your dog is more likely to obey an adult's voice.

Jesus didn't have any pets (that we know of). But when he spoke, the whole of creation listened.

Bible time: Read Mark 4:35-41

What was the result of Jesus speaking to the wind and the waves?

Who's the boss? Getting a dog to obey you is possible when you are its owner, or the person giving it treats. The dog wants to listen. But Jesus was able to get a **STORM** to obey him. How?!

Remember yesterday, when we learnt that Jesus was there in the beginning, when God created the world and spoke it into existence? And that God actually created the world **THROUGH** Jesus?

Get this: The storm obeyed Jesus because it recognised his voice from the creation of the world! Jesus had authority over the stormy wind and the crashing waves because he **MADE** them! They obeyed their master.

Take a moment to really think about that.

Peace vs fear: Notice the difference between Jesus and the disciples during the storm! Jesus was having a peaceful snooze, while the disciples were absolutely terrified.

But what's freakier than nearly drowning in a raging storm? Watching someone with the power to control that storm, as though the wind and waves had switches to flick on and off! The disciples just got a firsthand experience of what it means that Jesus really is God (verses 39-41)!

Jesus is with us in our storms: In the middle of their panic, feeling like they were drowning in a storm, the disciples forgot **WHO** was with them. Jesus, the one person who could do all kinds of miracles, was right there with them in the boat.

Jesus is with us in our "storms" too. The one person who can do **ALL** kinds of miracles is with us through our challenges, stressful moments and hard situations. We should call out to him! We can trust that Jesus is in control, even when things seem really tough.

Prayer prompt: Put yourself, or someone you care about, in this prayer.

Dear Jesus, this prayer is for (yourself or someone else)...

The "storm" (difficult situation) is...

I know you are in charge of everything because you are God. Can you please...

... and please help me to trust you if it seems like the "storm" is going on for a long time.

I pray this in your name. Amen.

5. Jesus Healed Someone With His Spit

If you have ever broken a bone or sprained a muscle, you'll know that recovering from those injuries isn't immediate. You may have to wear an unusual-looking boot or keep your arm in a sling. You might have to gradually strengthen your muscles with exercises until they work like they used to.

When Jesus healed people, it usually **WAS** immediate. Sometimes, though, there was quite an unusual process involved!

Bible time: Read John 9:1-11

How does Jesus describe himself in verse 5?

The backstory: The disciples mistakenly thought the man had been born blind because God was punishing some kind of sin. Jesus made it clear that this was not the case. In fact, the man was about to receive an extraordinary miracle from God. The light of the world was about to make a blind man see.

So about that miracle... As far as unusual remedies go, this one is up there! Jesus mixed his spit with some dirt to make mud, and put it on the man's eyes. **EEWWW!** Then he told the man to go to a certain pool and wash the mud off.

Why didn't Jesus just command the man's eyes to see? He could make a storm obey his voice, surely he could have made blindness do the same? Yes, Jesus could have. On another occasion (Mark 10:46-52), that's exactly what he chose to do. Jesus has authority to heal people however he wants—with or without mud!

And actually, Jesus **DID** use his voice. He told the man what to do to receive the gift of sight. Even though the man's healing wasn't immediate, it was still a miracle.

Seeing the truth: Some people, who knew that the man had been blind since birth, didn't want to see the truth of his healing. They didn't want to believe that Jesus had power to heal. They were spiritually blind to who Jesus really was—it was as if they had a murky darkness over their hearts, and they couldn't see God in the miracle.

Jesus **IS** the light of the world. When we look for him, we will be able to see the truth that Jesus really is God. When we open our hearts to him, we won't be spiritually blind. We can get to know Jesus, and learn how to follow him.

Prayer prompt: Reread verse 5 and sketch a picture of a light shining on a pathway or a Bible or your footsteps. Add Jesus' words from the verse. Ask Jesus to help you see who he really is, and understand how to follow him.

Week 5 Round-Up: What Only God Can Do

Let's recap some of the amazing things we found out about Jesus this week:

1. What did Jesus do when some friends broke through a roof to see him?
2. Which miraculous event was Jesus a part of, even before he was born as a baby?
3. Why did the furious storm obey Jesus' voice and calm down?

What's something important you learnt about Jesus this week?

What will you do to make that thing part of your life too?

A miracle is something only God can do. So, Jesus didn't just do these incredible things to make people's physical lives better—his miracles showed people that he is God the Son. Many believed in Jesus after seeing or experiencing one of his miracles.

Look up John 20:30-31. On one side of the book below, draw a picture of one of Jesus' amazing miracles. On the other side, use some words from verse 31 to form a statement about who you think Jesus really is. You could start with "I believe..."

Write a prayer and talk to God about something that's happened in your week or that's coming up in the week ahead.

See what great love the Father has lavished on us, that we should be called children of God! And that is what we are!

1 John 3:1a

Week 6
Jesus Always Gave More Than Enough

Do you know someone who is **SUPER**-generous? Perhaps they always share their best things with you, or give you extra time because they care about you. Maybe your family generously provides meals for others, or gives lots and lots and **LOTS** of hugs.

Generosity is an attitude of giving that spills out into actions.

Jesus' life was marked by acts of generosity. When he provided food, there were leftovers. When people were hurting, Jesus cared deeply. When an unpleasant job needed to be done, Jesus did it, so his friends didn't have to.

The generosity of Jesus was motivated by one thing: **LOVE.**

1. Jesus Invented Fast Food

What is your favourite kind of fast food? Whether it's pizza, sushi or a burger, sometimes it's just quicker and easier to grab a takeaway meal rather than cooking from scratch.

One time, when the disciples were worried about what to have for dinner, Jesus sorted it out with his own version of fast food.

Bible time: Read Matthew 14:13-21

How much food did the disciples have before they brought it to Jesus?

In the background: A crowd of 5,000 people had tracked Jesus down, even though he had gone looking for a place to be alone. When he saw the crowd, Jesus had compassion (a caring attitude) toward them.

An invitation: The disciples saw Jesus provide many miracles of healing that day. But when their rumbling tummies reminded them it was dinner time, they were ready for the miracles to be over. Jesus wasn't.

Check verse 16—Jesus, the miracle worker, invited his disciples to look for a solution to the food dilemma. The disciples could see one meal, but that wasn't enough. Where could they find more?

Bring it to Jesus: The disciples brought what they had to Jesus. Five loaves of bread and two fish must have seemed so small and insignificant compared to the huge, hungry crowd. But remember, Jesus helped create the **WHOLE WORLD** out of nothing! He could definitely make dinner for a crowd! The difference between a meal for one and a meal for 5,000 was Jesus!

When Jesus blesses it: First, Jesus gave thanks to God for the meal. Then he just kept handing food to the disciples—more and more and more! Jesus kept on providing. In fact, Jesus was so generous that there were more leftovers at the **END** of the meal than there was food to **START** with!

Sort the facts: Look back over the Bible reading and answer these questions:

- Which verse tells us that Jesus cares about people?
- What kind of prayer did Jesus say before the meal?
- Which verses remind us that Jesus can do miraculous things when we offer whatever we've got to him?

Jesus provides: It's God's nature to provide for us. In this story Jesus provided food for a hungry hoard, but soon he would provide something that would last much longer than one meal. The love and generosity of Jesus would provide the only way to salvation.

Prayer prompt: Be like Jesus. Give thanks to God for whatever he has provided for you—your food, your family, your life. And even if it seems kind of ordinary, remember Jesus can do miraculous things when we offer him whatever we've got.

2. Jesus Satisfied A Thirsty Person

Have you ever felt like an outsider? Perhaps you had to change schools, and it took a while to settle in. Or maybe you were the newbie in a sports team who were used to working together as a group.

When Jesus came across outsiders, he **ALWAYS** seemed to know how to welcome them in.

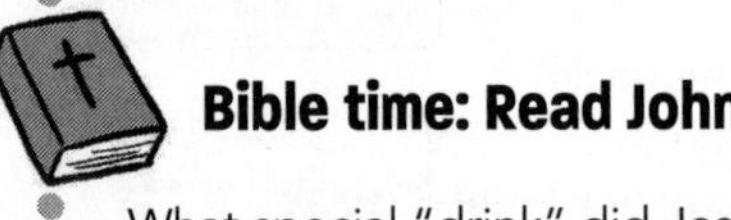

Bible time: Read John 4:4-14

What special "drink" did Jesus offer the Samaritan woman?

The backstory: We learnt in an earlier chapter that Samaritans and Jews did not get along. Yet here was Jesus, travelling through Samaria, chatting to a Samaritan woman. Can you tell by the Samaritan woman's conversation that there was tension in the air?

An outsider: In what way was the Samaritan woman an outsider? Wasn't Jesus the visitor here?

The Samaritan woman wasn't accepted by her own community. She came to get water from the well in the middle of the day, when it was really hot. Doing this meant she could avoid the other women from the town, who usually came at cooler times of the day. Later verses let us know that she was living a sinful life, which probably led others to exclude her.

The offer: Notice how Jesus turned the conversation around—from being about a drink of water to being about eternity! Jesus offered the woman a drink of something that would satisfy a need she didn't even know she had: salvation. Of course, it wasn't really a drink. Believing in Jesus is a life-giving choice that we can experience on earth, and later, in heaven forever.

Jesus knew this woman's story. He knew all the mistakes she had made—every sin, every bad choice. But he welcomed her into God's family anyway. She accepted the offer of living water.

Bible time: Read John 4:25-29

A new life: The woman, who seemed to be avoiding people from her town, was completely changed when she realised who Jesus was! She ran into town to tell **EVERYONE** that she had found the Messiah! She just **HAD** to share this good news!

The woman left her water jar behind at the well. Even though water is a physical need for every human being, the woman found something **BETTER.** She found living water that would satisfy her spiritual need.

Prayer prompt: Sketch a picture of a cup or drink bottle with water in it. Write a prayer thanking Jesus for offering us the life-giving opportunity to follow him.

3. Jesus Touched The Untouchable

When you're sick and have to stay home from school, it can feel like you're missing out. But because of the danger of spreading your germs to others and making them sick too, sometimes it's important to stay away.

When Jesus was on earth, there was a terrible skin disease called leprosy that had no cure. People who were diagnosed with leprosy had to isolate from their family and live with other lepers. No one was supposed to touch them in case they caught the disease themselves.

Bible time: Read Luke 5:12-13

What did Jesus do that showed he wasn't afraid of leprosy?

The backstory: What a horrible disease leprosy was! It gave you infectious sores on your skin, and there was no treatment for it. Lepers had to leave their homes, wear rags and call themselves "unclean".

Out of bounds: When the man with leprosy approached Jesus, he was **WAY** out of bounds! The law said he wasn't supposed to do that. Perhaps he risked it because he thought his life couldn't get any worse. As he begged Jesus for healing, he believed that Jesus **COULD** do it. But **WOULD** he?

In an interesting turn of events, Jesus also went out of bounds. He didn't **NEED** to touch the man in order to heal him. But in a moment of true compassion, Jesus gave more than what was required. He didn't stay at a distance. He touched the man most people treated as untouchable. The leper wasn't isolated from God's love!

Infectious: Jesus showed that his power to heal was more infectious than leprosy. That's what the man believed too: in his impossible situation, the power of Jesus could heal his body. But the man received a bonus! The love of Jesus healed his heart.

God reached out: This short story of healing reminds us of what God has done for us. Jesus lovingly reached out to touch a man who had been isolated because of his sickness. There was no other cure for him.

We might not be sick with leprosy, but the Bible says we have all been isolated from God because of our sin. We couldn't fix our sin problem ourselves, so God lovingly reached out to humanity, sending Jesus. He is willing and able to make us "clean" from our sin.

Prayer prompt: Just like the leper had to come to Jesus and ask to be made clean, so do we. Jesus loves you **SO** much! When we come to him, saying sorry for our sin, he will forgive us. Talk to Jesus now, asking him to make your heart "clean".

4. Jesus Cried Over A Friend

Do you have good friends you don't see very often? Maybe you keep in touch through video calls, or you catch up occasionally in your holidays. It's good to stay connected with friends you care about.

Jesus had many friends: the disciples, other followers, and one particular family he visited several times. Friendships were important to Jesus, just like they are to you. On this occasion, Jesus didn't immediately do what you might expect a good friend to do.

Bible time: Read John 11:3-7

Jesus didn't rush back to help his friend. What reason does he give in verse 4?

But... **OH NO!** When Jesus finally arrived at his friends' place, it seemed like he was too late. Lazarus had died.

Bible time: Now read John 11:32-44

Big emotions: Jesus is God, so he knew what was going to happen... but he was still overwhelmed with big emotions. The reality of his friend's death and the sadness of the grieving family still broke his heart. Jesus cried.

Was Jesus late or on time? People were watching Jesus to see how he would react. They were wondering why Jesus, the healer, hadn't arrived in time to heal his close friend... Or perhaps Jesus arrived right on time.

More than we think: Jesus didn't just randomly avoid his friends. We can tell by his tears that he **CARED** about Lazarus. But Jesus had a bigger miracle in mind. Imagine how much faith was required by Lazarus' two sisters to agree to open the grave, where Lazarus had been lying dead for four days! But it's a good thing they did!

We can trust Jesus more than we think. That doesn't mean everything we ask him for will happen. It means that even when things seem impossibly bad, we can trust that Jesus knows, he cares, he understands what it's like to hurt, and he has a much bigger picture in mind.

Responding to Jesus: This miracle, the resurrection of Lazarus, became very well known. Many people were full of amazement and glorified God, as Jesus said they would. They believed in Jesus. Others became so angry about what he was doing that they started plotting to kill him.

Either way, it was **IMPOSSIBLE** to ignore Jesus. So many miracles. So much power from God. So much wisdom in his words. So much love for others. How will **YOU** respond to Jesus?

Prayer prompt: One way to respond to Jesus is to praise him. This kind of prayer is not about us but all about God, expressing our awe and gratitude to him. It might start with, "Jesus, you are…"

5. Jesus Acted Like A Servant

Imagine you were going away for a long time. If you had just a few days to spend with your friends and family, what would you want to do with them? Go on a memorable adventure? Have a quiet day together just talking? Visit your favourite spots and eat special food together?

Jesus did some of these things when he was getting ready to leave the disciples. But he did something unexpected as well.

Bible time: Read John 13:1-15

What unusual thing did Jesus do for his disciples?

The timeline: These verses tell us that Jesus' time on earth was coming to a close. And the memorable thing he wanted to do with his special friends was… the grotty job of a servant. **WHAT?!?**

Back to front: The roads the disciples travelled on with Jesus were rough, dusty tracks. Instead of shoes, most people wore open sandals—so their feet often became very dirty and probably quite smelly! So **WHY** did Jesus do the lowly job of washing their feet? Why didn't he ask one of the others to do it?

Peter was uncomfortable with the idea of Jesus, the Son of God, washing his feet. He tried to protest. How could their Lord and master do a servant's task? It all seemed back to front! But Jesus insisted.

The character of Jesus: Jesus wanted his disciples to know that God's love **SERVES** others. This act, where Jesus stooped down to wash stinky, dirty feet, shows us Jesus' humility. It also gives us a preview of what Jesus would do on the cross—taking on the worst of punishments to cleanse us of our sin.

Check back on verse 13. Jesus **IS** Teacher and Lord. But being in charge doesn't mean bossing others around. Jesus showed us how to lead by loving and serving others. And he said we should follow his example.

What does it mean for me? Washing smelly feet is not a requirement to be a follower of Jesus. (**PHEW!**) But if Jesus is our Lord, then we should have the same attitude of serving others, loving others and humbly putting others first. This doesn't always come naturally to us! Maybe that's why Jesus made such a point of showing the disciples what humility means.

Prayer prompt: Think of ways you can love, serve and put others first. You could be extra kind to someone who is lonely, or you could let your sibling go first when it's really your turn. Write three things, then ask Jesus to help you have the right attitude when you do them.

I can love others by…

I can serve others by…

I can put others first by…

Week 6 Round-Up: Why Jesus Was So Generous

Let's recap the love and generosity of Jesus from this week.

1. What kind of food did Jesus miraculously multiply so that a crowd wouldn't go hungry?
2. Which disease did Jesus heal, that most people wouldn't have gone anywhere near?
3. How did Jesus show his disciples to love others by serving them?

What's something important you learnt about Jesus this week?

What will you do to make that thing part of your life too?

Jesus was so incredibly generous—and it was all to show what God is like! **WE** can also be generous and show God's love to others. In fact, Jesus commanded it! (Check John 13:34-35.)

That's a big call! Thankfully, Jesus gives us lots of examples of his love to follow, and he helps us to live out his command.

Look up 1 Corinthians 13:4-7. Which of these descriptions of love do you need God's help with? Choose three and write them in the hearts below. Then pray about each one. Remember, other people will see what Jesus is like if we can love others like Jesus loves us.

Write a prayer and talk to God about something that's happened in your week or that's coming up in the week ahead.

Very rarely will anyone die for a righteous person, though for a good person someone might possibly dare to die. But God demonstrates his own love for us in this: while we were still sinners, Christ died for us.

Romans 5:7-8

Week 7
The Best And Worst Week Ever

Have you ever had a day that was so amazing, you thought it was the best day ever? What about the opposite: have you ever had a day that left you wondering if things could **POSSIBLY** get any worse?

Jesus is about to have both. In the space of a week, an adoring crowd will turn nasty, friendships will change, loyalty will be questioned… and Jesus will fulfill his mission here on earth. He's getting ready to die.

As we focus on some of the events that happened in the week leading up to his crucifixion, just remember: Jesus **CHOSE** this.

1. Jesus Rode Through The Streets Like A King

When an Olympic Games team returns to their home country, there is often a huge parade in their honour. The athletes wear their medals to show their success, and people line the streets, cheering and waving and celebrating their victories.

Did you know that Jesus had a similar kind of parade, with people cheering and waving for him?

Bible time: Read John 12:12-19

What royal title did the crowd give Jesus as they called out?

The backstory: Crowds of Jewish people were gathering in the holy city, Jerusalem, for the yearly festival of Passover. But this time, the festival wasn't the only thing that people were interested in. Jesus had recently raised his friend Lazarus from the dead, which had caused quite a stir! After about three years of teaching, healing, and miraculous signs, Jesus was **FAMOUS!**

A right royal parade: People were waving palm branches and cheering. They were running in front of Jesus, throwing their coats down for the donkey to step on. They were chasing after him, calling out in excitement. They were treating Jesus like royalty.

Finally people were recognising it! Jesus **IS** royalty! He deserves this kind of honour!

Why now? The crowd came to get a glimpse of someone famous, but Jesus had a different purpose. In verse 14, John says, "Jesus found a young donkey and sat upon it, *as it is written*". Jesus was fulfilling a prophecy that said God's promised Messiah would ride a donkey's colt into Jerusalem. Jesus was declaring himself to be the Messiah, who would soon rescue the world.

A different kind of kingdom: Jesus **IS** royalty, but his is a different kind of kingdom. Jesus wasn't like the Roman rulers, who were harsh and demanding. He wasn't like the religious leaders, who thought they were better than others because of the rules they kept.

God's kingdom brings God's reign—his love, his justice, his power. Jesus **DID** come to save, but not in the way the cheering crowd hoped. His purpose wasn't to rescue them from the powerful Romans—he was going to rescue them from the power of sin. And the **WAY** he would carry out his purpose... well, that would be something even more **EXTRAORDINARY!!!**

Prayer prompt: King Jesus is worth celebrating! Draw a picture of a crown in the box below. Around the outside of the crown, fill the space with words of praise that honour Jesus, such as "Jesus is Lord of creation!" or "Thank you for being my Saviour".

2. Jesus Got Angry (For The Right Reason)

Are you someone who shows their emotions? Perhaps you cheer like crazy for your sports team and get upset if they lose, or maybe you lavish your pet with heaps of love and attention. We all have emotions, but some people show them more than others.

Jesus showed lots of emotions. Did you know that occasionally, Jesus even showed anger?

Bible time: Read Mark 11:15-18

What did Jesus say the temple (God's house) **SHOULD** be called?

The backstory: The city of Jerusalem was buzzing. It was full of visitors who had come for the Passover festival. It was full of tension. Some people were excited, believing that Jesus was the Messiah, while others were furious that he claimed to be the Son of God.

It was busy at the temple that day. During special festivals, people were required to offer animal sacrifices to God. It wasn't practical for travellers to bring live animals from a long distance, so they would buy them when they arrived. Sometimes they would need to exchange money to have the right coins for their offering. Everyone could conveniently get what they needed in one place: the temple courtyard.

So, why was Jesus angry? Remember how Jesus could read people's thoughts, and see what their real motivations were? The sellers and money changers at the temple seemed interested in over-charging to make a profit, rather than in providing a way for people to worship God. It was as if making money from buying and selling had become **THE** important business of the temple.

This wasn't what God's house was intended for. It dishonoured God.

Jesus was angry about what was happening at the temple. Instead of being a place of prayer and worship, it had become a place to cheat people. Jesus knew this was wrong! He couldn't just stand by and watch the sellers turn God's house into a den of robbers.

Jesus didn't sin in his anger; instead he honoured God by reminding people what God's house was intended for.

What God intended: Jesus quoted the Old Testament when he turfed out the sellers. Look up Isaiah 56:7, which talks about God's "house of prayer". What were people **MEANT** to experience in God's house?

Prayer prompt: Jesus' anger is sometimes called "holy anger"—because his motivation was to honour God, not to hurt people. Ask God to help you when you have big feelings. Pray that you will be able to honour God and obey him, no matter how you feel.

3. Jesus Asked His Friends To Be There For Him

Have you ever wrestled with a big decision, and weren't sure what to do? Perhaps, deep down, you knew what the right choice was, but you needed the strength and encouragement to actually do it. It's good to have friends and family to stand by you in those moments.

Jesus wrestled with a tough choice too. A terrible time was coming up, and he knew how hard it would be to follow through with it. So, Jesus asked his closest friends to be there for him.

Bible time: Read Matthew 26:36-46

Use your own words to describe how Jesus was feeling in verses 37-38.

The backstory: The disciples didn't know they had just had their last supper with Jesus. It was evening as they walked to a garden where Jesus liked to pray. Jesus was **REALLY** upset.

What was Jesus wrestling with? Why does Jesus talk about a "cup"? When Jesus prayed, the "cup" represented pain and death. He asked God if it was possible for him to avoid the brutal pain of crucifixion. He asked if there was a different way to save the world… but there wasn't. Jesus willingly obeyed and followed God's plan.

It's really important to understand that even though Jesus found it hard, he **CHOSE** to go to the cross.

Jesus prayed: Jesus knew his whole mission was about to come to a very ugly climax. He also knew that praying would help. Talking with

God his Father didn't change the outcome—Jesus still had to die—but after praying through the night, Jesus seemed to be comforted and strengthened, ready to face his accusers.

The problem with friends... Friends are great, usually. But we all make mistakes. That night, Jesus' three closest friends couldn't stay awake to be there for Jesus while he wrestled in prayer.

The benefit of friends... If Jesus asked his friends to support him in his toughest moments, so should we. One of the best ways we can do that is to ask others to pray with us. When we offer our Christian friends, family, and mentors the opportunity to partner with us in prayer, they get to bring the important moments in our lives to God, on our behalf! They get to stand by us in prayer.

Prayer prompt: Think about something that is on your mind to pray for. It may be a big decision, or a small ongoing issue. Who will you ask to pray with you or pray for you?

Write it down, like a note, and then get a message to that person, asking them to partner with you in prayer.

Dear ...

Please pray with me for...

4. Jesus Walked Into A Trap

Are you one of those people who likes to hide in a sneaky spot, to jump out and give someone a fright? Or are you more likely to be the victim of this kind of setup, yelling out in fright with embarrassing loudness? This kind of trap only works if it is a surprise.

Most people wouldn't walk into an unpleasant situation by choice. But that's what Jesus did, and this was definitely not a game!

Bible time: Read Mark 14:42-50, then verses 66-72

How did Jesus' disciples let him down that night?

The betrayal: This story continues on immediately from yesterday. After praying through the night, Jesus was ready for what was coming next. Even so, it must have been deeply distressing when Judas—one of Jesus' disciples—led soldiers to arrest him.

And that was just the start. Betrayed, arrested, accused, deserted, denied. Have you ever wondered why Jesus didn't cut short his prayer time and go and hide somewhere, instead of letting Judas find him in the garden?

The denial: Then there's Peter—one of Jesus' closest friends! Jesus had predicted Peter's denial. Sure enough, Peter's fear of being arrested himself meant he disowned his faith and his friend.

The trap: Judas thought **HE** came up with the plan to entrap Jesus, but did he?

Remember how Jesus had been wrestling in prayer about the pain and suffering he was about to go through? This was part of it. Jesus knew what was going to happen.

Wait, he **KNEW?!** And he still followed through with it?

Jesus knew all of it. He knew Judas would betray him. He knew Peter would disown him. He warned the disciples. As all his friends deserted him, Jesus never deserted his mission to save the world. Jesus would be crucified to forgive the sins that were unfolding right in front of him. He would die as an act of love, even when people didn't love him back. That's the generosity of Jesus.

It might look like Jesus walked into a trap, but he **DIDN'T.** He walked into God's plan. The **ONLY** plan that could save us.

When the rooster crowed: Roosters crow at the dawn of a new day. That means Jesus had been awake all night: praying, then arrested, questioned and beaten. The new day was Friday. A week earlier, Jesus was cheered into Jerusalem as king. Now he's under arrest like a criminal. And things are about to go from bad to worse.

Prayer prompt: As you dwell on what happened in the lead-up to Jesus' crucifixion, bring your awe and your thankfulness to Jesus.

5. Jesus Was Silent

There are certain times when respectful quietness, or even silence, is required. Some people find this easy, because they prefer not to talk too much. Others find it very hard!

When Jesus was on trial, the religious leaders asked him many times to answer their accusations. After teaching large crowds with godly wisdom and doing incredible miracles, it's what Jesus **DIDN'T** do that is so surprising. When he **COULD** have defended himself, the greatest teacher of all time remained quiet.

Bible time: Read Mark 15:1-15

What did Pilate call Jesus?

The backstory: During Thursday night and all Friday morning, Jesus was on trial in front of different "rulers": religious leaders, Jewish high priests and Roman officials.

The Jewish religious leaders, who wanted Jesus dead, didn't have the power to enact the death penalty. That's why they needed the local Roman ruler, Pilate, to approve it.

On trial: Jesus was on trial for claiming to be the Son of God (which he is). Even after three years of amazing miracles, the hard-hearted religious leaders could not see who Jesus really was.

Pilate knew Jesus didn't deserve death, but he was trying to avoid a riot. He wasn't really concerned about doing what was right. Yet he was amazed that Jesus didn't defend himself against the Jewish leaders.

Who's in charge? You might think that now would be the perfect time for Jesus to pull out a miracle—to prove he was God and show all those "leaders" who was **REALLY** in charge!

He could have. Jesus had the power to command weather, sickness and death to obey him. If he'd wanted to, Jesus could have defended himself with powerful words and actions. But he chose **NOT** to. Instead, he followed God's plan and didn't resist the people who thought they were in control.

What IS the plan? Considering that Jesus' mission was to save the world, dying might not seem like a very effective plan.

Actually, it was the **PERFECT** plan. Jesus never sinned, so by offering himself as a sacrifice, he could take the punishment for **ALL** sin. Just as one act of disobedience from Adam and Eve first brought sin into the world, one act of obedience from Jesus broke the power of sin in the world. That was the plan all along.

So, Jesus had to die. The most innocent man who ever lived was sentenced to a criminal's death.

Prayer prompt: Find a timer and set it for one minute. Observe a minute of silence and stillness in memory of what Jesus did. In your mind, honour Jesus for the choice he made to submit to God's plan, despite what it cost him.

Week 7 Round-Up: God's Plan in Motion

Let's reflect on the last week of Jesus' life with a quick quiz.

1. Describe what the crowd was doing when Jesus rode into Jerusalem as King.
2. What emotion did Jesus feel when he saw people making dishonest money instead of worshipping God in the temple?
3. Describe how Jesus felt when he was praying at night in the garden.

What a rollercoaster of emotions Jesus' final week was! But all of it—**ALL OF IT**—was part of God's plan.

What's something important you learnt about Jesus this week?

What will you do to make that thing part of your life too?

Here is a prophecy about God's promised Messiah, written hundreds of years before Jesus was born. Circle or highlight anything you can find that links with the events of the week we've just read about.

We all have wandered away like sheep.
Each of us has gone his own way.
But the Lord has put on him the punishment
for all the evil we have done.
He was beaten down and punished.
But he didn't say a word.
He was like a lamb being led to be killed.
He was quiet, as a sheep is quiet while its wool is being cut.
He never opened his mouth.
Men took him away roughly and unfairly.
He died without children to continue his family.
He was put to death.
He was punished for the sins of my people.
He was buried with wicked men.
He died with the rich.
He had done nothing wrong.
He had never lied. (Isaiah 53:6-9, ICB)

Write a prayer and talk to God about something that's happened in your week or that's coming up in the week ahead.

If you declare with your mouth, "Jesus is Lord," and believe in your heart that God raised him from the dead, you will be saved.

Romans 10:9

Week 8
Jesus Gave His Life For Us

Have you ever done a trade with someone? Perhaps you swapped collectable cards with a friend, or you traded chores with your sibling at home. Usually, people agree to trade when it's a fair exchange—the value of what you swap is similar.

When Jesus died, an exchange was made. We sinned, but Jesus (who never sinned) took the punishment for it. That's not a fair trade—in fact, it seems remarkably **UN**fair!

But God knew we couldn't save ourselves from sin. In his great love for us, God sent Jesus to live a perfect life, to die a sacrificial death, **AND** to come back to life to save us!

The far-reaching power of Jesus' **MOST AMAZING** miracle is about to be revealed!

1: Jesus Died

Have you ever been asked to forgive someone when you weren't really sure you wanted to? Perhaps you remembered the way they hurt your feelings, or maybe you weren't convinced they were sorry for what they did.

Forgiving people can be hard. Even as Jesus died, forgiveness was on his mind.

Bible time: Read Luke 23:32-46

The death of Jesus is an incredibly sad moment. As Jesus hung on the cross, who did he forgive and promise a place in heaven (or "paradise")?

What happened: Crucifixion is a brutal way to die. Jesus' body felt as much pain and suffering as anyone else's body would. Plus, as he was dying, people laughed and insulted him.

Signs of power: If it seems like Jesus' miraculous power has deserted him, remember: Jesus **CHOSE** to die as part of God's plan. He was still as powerful as ever—he just didn't use his power to save himself. He used it to save **US.**

Other strange signs happened too. Instead of sunlight, there was darkness. And a huge temple curtain was mysteriously ripped apart. This curtain was about 9cm or 3-and-a-half inches thick. That's thicker than most carpets!

About that curtain... It might seem odd to mention some fabric at this life-or-death moment. But there is a reason the temple curtain is so significant.

The heavy curtain blocked off a special part of the temple where God's presence was. Only the high priest was permitted to go into that most holy place once a year, to make a sacrifice for people's sin and ask God's forgiveness on their behalf. No one else was allowed in. **EVER.** The curtained-off area symbolised God's holiness, and our separation from him because of our sin.

When Jesus died, the power of sin was broken. Because of his sacrifice, Jesus made a way for us to go straight to God and ask for forgiveness ourselves. We don't have to stay separated from God because of sin! The curtain was no longer required, so God tore it up!

The cross: We know that Jesus' sacrifice on the cross was the **ONLY** way for us to be forgiven, and we should remember what it cost him to do this.

Sketch the outline of a cross and write **I AM FORGIVEN** in the cross shape. Add **JESUS DIED FOR ME** along the top of the picture.

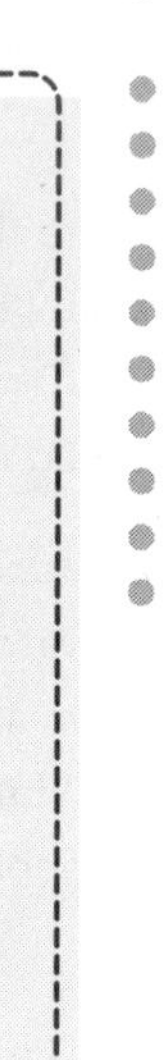

Prayer prompt: Look at your sketch with an attitude of thankfulness to Jesus. Ask him for forgiveness if there's anything you know you should say sorry for. Thank him for laying down his life for you.

2. Jesus Came Back To Life!

Have you ever been totally shocked by some unexpected, exciting news? Like, mouth-hanging-open, unable-to-speak, knock-your-socks-off news?

Jesus' friends were about to experience that mixture of shock and joy!

Bible time: Read Luke 24:1-8, then skip to verses 36-44

Which words in these two scenes describe how Jesus' friends were feeling?

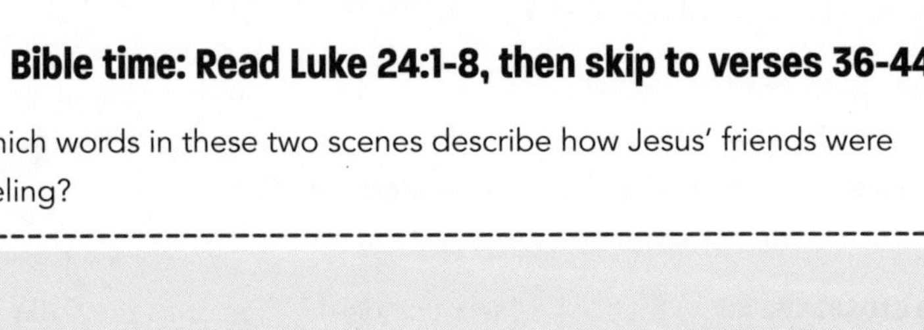

The backstory: Jesus died on a Friday afternoon. His body was taken down from the cross and placed in a tomb (like a cave), with a large stone sealing the entrance. The next day was the Sabbath—the day of rest—so no one could care for the body until Sunday.

Remember...? The women who went to the tomb were expecting to find a dead body, but there wasn't one! How was that possible? Angels (that's the men in clothes like lightning) reminded the frightened women about what Jesus had told them. Could it be **TRUE?!?**

Then Jesus himself appeared to the stunned disciples! He really was alive! After convincing them that he wasn't a ghost, Jesus reminded them of his teaching: it was God's plan all along for Jesus to die and come back to life. God had even left hints through prophecies in the Old Testament about what would happen to Jesus (verse 44). God's plan had been fulfilled!

God's power: By coming back to life, Jesus proved once and for all that he really is God. Acts 2:24 says, "It was impossible for death to keep its hold on him". That's because Jesus is more powerful than death! His resurrection destroyed the power of sin and death **FOREVER.**

Through Jesus, forgiveness of sin is available to **EVERYONE** who believes in him. That means we can be friends with God now, and have eternal life with him in heaven after we die.

The miracle that keeps on giving: The 2,000-year-old miracle of Jesus' resurrection is an ongoing promise for us all. It's powerful enough to forgive every sin of every person—whoever believes in him. Only Jesus could have achieved that!

Jesus is alive again! Choose a fact from today's study that sums up Jesus' powerful resurrection, like "Jesus is more powerful than death!" or simply "Jesus is alive!" Write it in the shape using bright colours, as a reminder of Jesus' powerful resurrection.

Prayer prompt: It's praise time! The disciples felt joy and amazement when they spent time with the risen Jesus. We can too. Let Jesus know how awesome and powerful you think he is!

3. Jesus Restores

Do you like to watch the same movies over and over again, even if you are familiar with the storyline? If you have a favourite movie, you may even be able to recite the best lines word for word!

The disciples were about to experience a re-run of familiar events. Do you remember when Jesus first invited the fishermen, including Simon Peter, to follow him? If you do, the first part of this story might sound strangely familiar...

Bible time: Read John 21:3-8, then skip to verses 14-19

How many times did Jesus ask Simon Peter about his love?

The backstory: The disciples believed that Jesus had come back to life, but they weren't quite sure what to do next. This repeat miracle reminded them that Jesus was **STILL** the Messiah. Their job was **STILL** to follow him.

A private chat: After the disciples ate a meal together, Jesus had a private conversation with Simon Peter. This was a very different kind of re-run, and one that Simon Peter may have preferred to avoid.

On the night that Jesus was betrayed and arrested, Peter hadn't been a very good friend to Jesus. In fact, he had failed Jesus badly. He declared three times that he didn't know Jesus, didn't follow him, didn't believe in him. When Peter realised his terrible mistake, he was **HEARTBROKEN.** Then Jesus died.

Now that Jesus was alive again, it might seem awkward that he singled out Peter to question his loyalty. It probably was! It's no coincidence that Jesus gave Peter three opportunities to declare his love and faithfulness.

From failure to forgiveness: Jesus died for this. He died so that Peter (and all of us) could be completely forgiven. There is no failure so big, and no sin so bad, that Jesus' death and resurrection can't forgive it.

Restored: Jesus didn't just forgive Peter—he deliberately took him aside so their friendship could be restored, or put back to the way it should be. That's how forgiveness from God works! Jesus even trusted Peter with an important leadership task in the church, looking after the "sheep", meaning Jesus' followers.

What does it mean for me? Instead of pretending we haven't made mistakes, God would rather we admit our failures and say sorry for them. That means saying sorry to people we may have hurt **AND** saying sorry to God. Yes, that can be awkward, but it's the way to forgiveness—and the way to put right our relationship with God and others.

Prayer prompt: Take this opportunity to declare your love for Jesus. Say sorry for any sins you may have tried to ignore, and ask Jesus to forgive you, so your friendship with him (and maybe with others) can be fully restored.

If you have never asked Jesus to forgive your sin and invited him to be your Saviour, on page 125 there is a prayer that will help your friendship with Jesus to be fully restored.

4. Jesus Gave Us A Mission

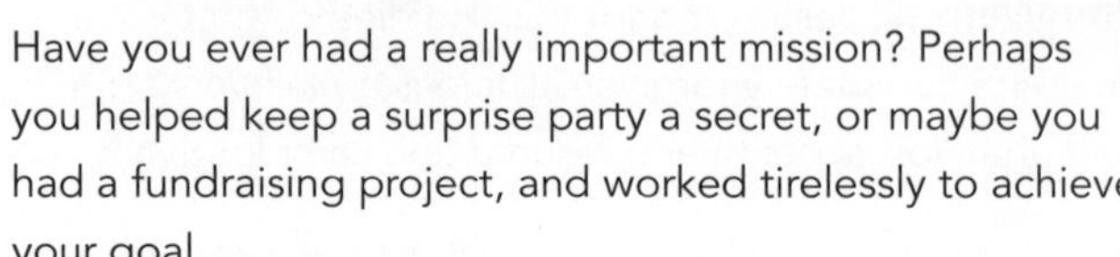

Have you ever had a really important mission? Perhaps you helped keep a surprise party a secret, or maybe you had a fundraising project, and worked tirelessly to achieve your goal.

Jesus came to earth on a mission to save the world, and he had done his part. **NOW** what?

Bible time: Read Matthew 28:16-20

Who did Jesus say they should go and make disciples of?

Where are we up to? Jesus died and came back to life, appearing to many of his followers. His perfect life, sacrificial death and powerful resurrection proved he was God's Son. His mission—to destroy the power of sin and save the world through an act of love—was complete.

Changing it up: Jesus was about to give the disciples a bit of a surprise. You see, even though he had just said he would always be with them, it wasn't going to be the same as before. Jesus was about to go back to heaven, leaving the disciples with the responsibility of telling the rest of the world the good news of what he had done.

Not alone: Jesus' mission had to continue—**WITHOUT** him. This was the last thing he told his followers before he returned to heaven. But God the Son didn't leave them to do it alone: God the Holy Spirit would help them! You can check out what Jesus said about this in Acts 1:8-9.

Go! Jesus isn't just making a suggestion when he says, "Go and make disciples"—he's pretty firm about it! You could say it sounds like a command!

The instruction to **BE** disciples who **MAKE** disciples doesn't end with those eleven men who were with Jesus in his final days. Reread Matthew 28:18-20, but this time, imagine Jesus is talking to **YOU.**

Our part in the story: A disciple of Jesus is someone who believes in him, learns from him and lives like him. It's up to each individual person to choose to say **YES** to the saving power of Jesus and become his disciple.

Then it's up to his disciples (that's **US**) to go and tell others. But we don't go on our own. We go in the authority of Jesus, empowered by the Holy Spirit. We don't have to know everything about God in order to share his love. We don't have to wait until we are older before we tell others what Jesus has taught us.

If you are a disciple of Jesus, you have a part in his story!

Prayer prompt: Ask Jesus to give you the courage to be a disciple who makes disciples. If you like, you could write down the names of some people you would like to share Jesus' love with. Pray for them and ask for the Holy Spirit's help!

5. Jesus Sent Help

"How can I help you?"

Has someone ever asked you that question when you were at a shop counter, the doctor's or the library? The person's job is to match you with the help you need.

Jesus knew the disciples would need help when he went back to heaven. After all, he had given them quite a task! Jesus promised that help would come, and he knew **EXACTLY** who to send.

Bible time: Read Acts 2:1-8

How were the disciples able to speak in different languages?

All the nations: Pentecost was a festival that happened 50 days after Passover. Jews had gathered in Jerusalem from different nations to celebrate, including the disciples.

Do you remember from yesterday that Jesus commanded his disciples to tell **ALL THE NATIONS** about him? Just in case the disciples were wondering how that would work, at Pentecost God provided people from other nations and the power to speak to them in their own languages! God the Holy Spirit, the promised helper, had arrived!

Just to recap: The disciples spoke languages they had never learnt! Tongues of **FIRE** landed on people's heads, but they weren't burnt! There was also a loud, powerful windstorm **INSIDE** the house! A confused passerby asked a good question in Acts 2:12: "What does this **MEAN?**"

Bible backstory: We know the Holy Spirit has always existed—he's mentioned in the story of creation (Genesis 1:2). Throughout the Old Testament, God's Spirit came upon certain individuals God had chosen. The Holy Spirit empowered them to fulfill God's work, like performing miracles, prophesying or leading his people.

When Jesus died and came back to life, he broke the power of sin that separated us from God. Now, **EVERY** believer gets God's Holy Spirit to always be with them! We don't have to live out our faith in our own strength—we have God's strength **IN** us!

God's Holy Spirit: The Holy Spirit isn't a human person, like Jesus, but he is just as real. The Bible tells us that God's Holy Spirit is our helper, comforter and spiritual guide, and we can tell from today's Bible reading that God's Spirit brings God's miraculous power!

Even though Jesus had gone back to heaven, the disciples now knew that God was still with them… but even closer than before. Now God (the Holy Spirit) was **IN** them!

Prayer prompt: God's Holy Spirit empowered the disciples to continue Jesus' mission. Draw a flame and write around the outside, "God's power is in me to continue Jesus' mission". Thank God that his Spirit is always with you.

Week 8 Round-Up: It's Not Really The End...

Let's think back on what we've learnt with a quick quiz:

1. Which of these is more powerful: death or Jesus?
2. How would people find out about Jesus' mission, when he returned to heaven?
3. Who would empower them to tell others about Jesus?

What's something important you learnt about Jesus this week?

What will you do to make that thing part of your life too?

Jesus' ministry wasn't over when he went back to heaven. In fact, because Jesus sent the Holy Spirit, something new sparked to life!

Read Acts 2:14, then verses 36-39. This is the **SAME** Peter who failed Jesus when he was afraid. Now he is preaching to a huge crowd and telling them how to be saved. What a change! That's what God's Spirit in us can do!

Imagine that someone asked **YOU** what they needed to do to be saved. What would you say? Look back at what Peter said, and use your own words to tell them how to become a disciple of Jesus.

Write a prayer and talk to God about something that's happened in your week or that's coming up in the week ahead.

Bye For Now...

Even though we've come to the end of this devotional book about Jesus, your journey with him doesn't have to end here. In fact, I hope it continues for a very long time! Reading the Bible and talking to Jesus every day is a great habit to keep up.

And there are so many **MORE** stories, miracles, teachings and opportunities to get to know Jesus in the Bible. A good way to continue might be by reading the book of Acts. That's where those ordinary fishermen (Jesus' disciples) learn to live out what Jesus taught them, after he had gone back to heaven.

Jesus really is the Greatest Of All Time—the greatest teacher, the greatest miracle worker, the greatest friend, the greatest (and only) saviour. And the best part: he really wants to be **YOUR** teacher, **YOUR** friend, and **YOUR** Saviour.

You see, it's personal. Jesus became human like us, because he loves us, so he could save us. And all any of us has to do is choose to put our trust in him.

Spoiler alert: It's the greatest choice you could ever make!

The G.O.A.T. and Me (How To Become A Disciple Of Jesus)

"Becoming a Christian", "inviting Jesus into your heart", or "asking Jesus to be your Lord and Saviour"—these phrases all describe the same thing using different words. Whichever way you say it, you can become a disciple of Jesus.

This is a choice anyone can make, but no one else can choose it for you. Whether you've always gone to church with your family or you're the only one in your family who wants to follow Jesus, there comes a point where **YOU** have to decide what Jesus means to you.

If you've never personally chosen to follow Jesus, but you'd like to, then on the next page is a prayer you can pray, with some Bible verses to look up. If you'd rather, you could use your own words to talk to God about becoming a disciple of Jesus. It's not about getting the words "right", it's about believing that Jesus can make your relationship with God right.

Dear God,

Thank you that you made me and you love me. (Romans 5:8)

I know I make the wrong choice sometimes and I have turned away from you so often. Please forgive me for my sin. (Romans 3:23)

Thank you, Jesus, that you died on the cross and came back to life again. I believe you paid the price for my sin, so I can have a restored, eternal friendship with you. I want you to be my Saviour and my friend. (John 3:16; Romans 10:9)

Please fill me with your Holy Spirit, the Helper, to be with me always and to remind me how to be a disciple of Jesus. Please help me do what you want me to do. (John 14:26)

Thanks God! You're awesome!

Amen.

PS: If you prayed that prayer for the first time, there's a party in heaven right now because of you (Luke 15:7)! Make sure you let someone know that you made your greatest choice ever today.

Jesus The G.O.A.T. Puzzle

Go to thegoodbook.com/alltime-puzzle to check your answers!

Across

1. One of the items of food that Jesus multiplied to feed a crowd.
4. Jesus showed his emotions when a good friend died. He _________.
8. Jesus was resurrected, which means he came back to _________!
9. Stories Jesus told that taught people spiritual truths.
14. Jesus sent a helper to always be with us. His name is God the _________ _________.
15. Jesus gave this age group a high priority.
17. The tax collector Zacchaeus climbed one of these to see Jesus.
19. Jesus told this type of bad weather to calm down.
20. Jesus was tempted by Satan but he never _________.
22. Jesus upset some "rule-keepers" when he did this on the Sabbath.
23. The king who was upset to learn that a NEW king had been born.
24. Jesus commanded his disciples to ______ and make more disciples.
25. Jesus' age when his parents thought they had lost him in Jerusalem.
26. A title for Jesus meaning the promised one, the Saviour.

Down

2. Jesus left this place to be born on earth.
3. The brutal way that Jesus died.
5. An important thing that Jesus did often, especially when he was alone.
6. The kind of tree branch that people waved when Jesus rode into Jerusalem like a king.
7. Jesus' cousin was known as John the __________.
10. Some of Jesus' disciples worked as _________ before they started following him.
11. Jesus died for us because he ________ us so much.
12. Jesus did many of these, to heal people and show he really was God.
13. Jesus said he had authority to forgive _________.
16. Jesus served his disciples by washing these.
18. A character trait shown by the good Samaritan.
21. No one forced Jesus to go to the cross—he _________ to do it.

BIBLICAL | RELEVANT | ACCESSIBLE

At The Good Book Company, we are dedicated to helping Christians and local churches grow. We believe that God's growth process always starts with hearing clearly what he has said to us through his timeless word—the Bible.

Ever since we opened our doors in 1991, we have been striving to produce Bible-based resources that bring glory to God. We have grown to become an international provider of user-friendly resources to the Christian community, with believers of all backgrounds and denominations using our books, Bible studies, devotionals, evangelistic resources, and DVD-based courses.

We want to equip ordinary Christians to live for Christ day by day, and churches to grow in their knowledge of God, their love for one another, and the effectiveness of their outreach.

Call us for a discussion of your needs or visit one of our local websites for more information on the resources and services we provide.

Your friends at The Good Book Company

thegoodbook.com | thegoodbook.co.uk
thegoodbook.com.au | thegoodbook.co.nz